COMPETING

COMPETING
Understanding and Winning the Strategic Games We All Play

Harvey L. Ruben, M.D., M.P.H.

LIPPINCOTT & CROWELL, PUBLISHERS / NEW YORK

ACKNOWLEDGMENTS

With gratitude and sincere appreciation I acknowledge the input, support, and help of Elizabeth McKee Purdy, Tad Tuleja, Lawrence Daskal, and Arnold Dolin and the staff at Lippincott & Crowell.

Patients' names and case histories have been changed to prevent identification and ensure confidentiality.

FIRST EDITION

Designed by Ginger Legato

U.S. Library of Congress Cataloging in Publication Data

Ruben, Harvey L
   Competing: understanding and winning the strategic games we all play.
   Includes index.
   1. Competition (Psychology) I. Title.
BF637.C47R8   158'.1   79-24997
ISBN 0-690-01873-8

80 81 82 83 84 10 9 8 7 6 5 4 3 2 1

In memory of my father, Milton,
who first taught me about competition,
and in honor of my newest son, Marc.
May he profit from the insights I have gained.

Contents

Part III: A Competitor's Primer

INTRODUCTION:
Playing the Game Your Way

Competition is an inescapable fact of life.

From the nursery to the nursing home, from the bedroom to the boardroom, in politics and business and school and sports and everyday conversation, human beings are in constant competition with each other. We compete for jobs, grades, social position, sex, friendship, money, power, even love. So pervasive is the competitive urge that it frequently governs our behavior even when we are unaware of its influence. From the time we are very small, it is a fundamental aspect of the process by which we develop our self-esteem, our social assurance, our very identity.

Of course, different people and different cultures deal with competitive behavior in different ways, but I think it's safe to say that the anthropologists have not yet discovered a single society from which competition, however much it may be despised, has been entirely eliminated. This is as true of the highly industrialized, even socialist societies as it is of traditional rural ones. The dream of a noncompetitive world, then, is simply that: a dream. For as long as men and women have walked the earth, they have vied with each other to win.

Is this healthy or unhealthy? The virtues and vices of competition have been debated for centuries, and yet so far no one has come up with incontrovertible evidence that the urge to win is either entirely beneficial or entirely detrimental to us. Social Darwinists are convinced that, in society as in nature, competition is the very lifeblood of self-preservation; due to the universal striving to win, they say, the survival of the fittest is assured. But many social scientists disagree, and philosophers from ancient times until today have felt that the urge to win is little more than a "softer" form of aggression; to them the universality of competitive urges in modern society is a sign not of health but of masked animalism and brutality.

I would not presume to think that I could untangle this knot of disagreement here. The ultimate value—or lack of value—of competition I will leave to the moral philosophers. I am a psychiatrist, and what concerns me is the psychological effect that the urge to win has on each of us. From my vantage point, it's obvious that competition is neither all good nor all bad. It is simply a fact of human life, and one that must be confronted, on an almost daily basis, if we are to establish any level of emotional well-being for ourselves, our friends, our children.

It's clear that learning to compete successfully is an integral part of human ego-development, and that many children who fail to learn how to compete early in life develop serious emotional problems later on. A sense of self-respect and esteem is central to the development of a healthy emotional constitution, and for better or worse, the way most of us gain that essential self-respect is by competing successfully with our peers. For the unfortunate person who cannot compete well, competition becomes a terrible hurdle, an obstacle which elicits nothing but unhealthy, self-destructive urges and desires. The successful competitor can often feel like a winner even when he loses, while the person who is accustomed to feeling like a loser will feel that way even when he wins.

This means that, in terms of mental health, it is generally more important to learn how to *compete* than how to *win*. In other words, "It's not whether you win or lose, but how you play the game." That is not simply a piece of conventional moralizing; while it refers to form and sportsmanship, it also speaks directly to the need that all of us have to feel good about ourselves. Since nobody can possibly win all the time, it's far more crucial, psychologically, to learn how to play competitive games well than it is to simply add up a string of victories. Victory, as we shall see, is often a state of mind.

How can we learn to play well? By way of answering that question, I want to relate an incident which happened to me when

I was very young—an incident which gave me my first, and still my most important, lesson about how to compete.

The summer I was eight, my best friend was a boy named Billy, and our favorite game was playing Indian. There was a small creek near where we lived, and we would spend hours there each day, skulking behind trees and talking to each other in monosyllables, as we had seen the Indians in the movies do. Our days together, in that idyllic time, were exceptionally carefree and close.

Until the new kid came along.

His name was Gary, and he was a year older and a couple of inches taller than we were. When he moved onto the block, we quickly discovered that "real" Indians were a lot more bloodthirsty than we had supposed.

As soon as Gary joined us at the creek, our playing became more violent, with roughhousing and daredevil stunts such as jumping out of trees the order of the day. Gary informed us that this was the way Indians played, and that we were sissies if we thought they liked fishing and hiding and grunting.

Now, I was not exactly Ruben the Boy Wonder. I had just undergone a growth spurt—in a lateral rather than vertical direction—and my physical powers were somewhat less than superhuman. As a result, not only did I have to share my friend, but I was unable to compete with either Gary or Billy in the feats of derring-do demanded by the new rules. I was always the last one up the tree, the last one across the stream, the one on the bottom in the wrestling match.

I endured these indignities for a couple of weeks, resigning myself to being low man on the totem pole, until one day something clicked inside of me. Where it came from I don't know, but it was a vague yet inescapable recognition that I had had enough. Suddenly I realized I had a *choice*. I didn't have to let Gary bully me out of my fun. I could do what *I* wanted to do, not what he told me I should be doing. I could play my own game.

So one day—knowing very well that I was risking losing Billy as well as Gary as a friend—I simply refused to go along. Gary had just challenged me to a wrestling match, and, still stunned by the realization that I could say no, I declined.

"You know I can't beat you," I said. "And I'm sick of trying. You do what you want. I'm going fishing."

And I walked away.

Neither of them followed me, and I had a pretty bad time of it that night. I felt I had gambled and lost. I knew it was the end of the idyll, and the end of my friendship with Billy too.

But the next morning I was awakened by a familiar sound. A shout of "Hey, Harveee . . ." came from the driveway, and when I looked out the window, there were Billy and Gary with fishing poles over their shoulders. For the rest of the summer we compromised, roughhousing when the mood struck us and fishing when it did not.

That incident taught me a valuable lesson. Somehow, simply by sticking to what I had wanted to do, I had won out over a stronger and older rival. That was my first inkling of a central competitive principle:

The only time you have any real chance of success is when you play the game your own way.

As I reflected on that summer in later years, I realized that the incident at the creek was a kind of prototype of the competitive situations we all confront every day. The more I thought about it, the more I saw how well it illustrated the fact that, in any given situation, you and only you can really determine how to play. If you size up your own assets and liabilities well, then trust that what you want to do is the best thing for you, you can hardly fail to come out ahead. Had I given in to Gary's taunts and tried to beat him at *his* game, I would certainly have lost out. As it was, relying on my own needs helped me to regain both my friend and my self-respect.

The number of people who consistently play other people's games is staggering. As a psychiatrist, I am always confronted by people who allow themselves to be coerced into competing in situations in which they know they can only end up as losers. They have not learned a fundamental competitive lesson: that winners are very often simply people who make it a point to decide when and where they will play, and when they will say "No, thanks."

Patients come to me every day seeking help for specific complaints. Their stories people this book. They suffer from anxiety, depression, frustration, anger, guilt—or from physical symptoms such as headaches, loss of appetite, nausea, and sexual difficulties. But what often underlies these problems is a lack of success in some competitive area—usually the social, family, or business area. Discussion generally reveals that, without being aware of it, they have let competition become a constantly debilitating aspect of their lives. They have fallen into patterns of letting other people tell them how and when to play, and so they feel constantly at a loss.

They know that competition is important. What they don't know is when to compete and when not to.

It's surprising how many emotional problems can be traced to this root cause. Inside many of us, it seems, there is a chubby kid who hates wrestling but insists on going to the mat again and again because somebody else—a parent, a teacher, a boss—has convinced him that it's the only game in town. In a culture as firmly competitive as ours, this unwillingness to change the rules, to walk away, to play our own games rather than those others present us with, creates many personal tragedies.

Confusion about how and when to compete seems to be almost as widespread as competition itself, and it was to clarify this issue that I began to write the present book. It's my hope that it will provide some useful insights into basic human behavior and that it will provide at least a partial answer to the perplexing questions concerning success and competition.

I say "partial" advisedly. I did not want to write just another self-help book, and yet I realized that some people would buy a book on competition hoping for a shortcut or prescription for happiness. Some would be looking for tricks, instant methods, clichés. Others would want to know only how to win. Many would be searching for the panacea which would work where all others had failed.

I would not want to deny that this book might help you achieve greater success or happiness in your life. But these are not quite synonymous with learning how to win, and if for you winning is the only thing that matters, then this book will probably not teach you very much. My intention is to help you understand the *nature* and *effects* of competition in your life. Ideally, what you will learn is how to weigh your own limitations and assets—as I did that summer by the creek—and how to use such knowledge to your advantage. You may or may not learn how to *win;* but you will learn how and when to *compete.*

In other words, I cannot promise you that, after reading this book, you will never again fall out of a tree, or fail to get a job you want, or lose a race that means a great deal to you. I *can* promise that, if you do fail, you'll be better able to size up the situation rationally, and then decide whether it's best to give it another try or say "To hell with this, I'll try something else."

Competition is unavoidable. Every one of us meets it every day. But not everybody can be a champion wrestler, a company president, or a social lion. Had I insisted on competing out of my league back at the creek, I might still be reaching for truly impossible dreams. That is what many of us do, consistently, and in spite of the blandishments of the Don Quixote myth, the "impossible dream" is not a healthy goal, for the result of attempts to attain it can often be tragic.

I'm not saying that success is unimportant, or that losing and winning are the same thing. But most of us allow others to determine both the style and the intensity of our competitive efforts, and that makes us losers, often, even when we appear to have won.

The only real success, then, is internal. What I hope this book can show you is that each of us must develop his or her own personal blueprint for success. In doing that, an understanding of the wisdom of a withdrawal or a shift from an unproductive competitive effort is often just as important as an appreciation of the excitement of success.

If you can understand when to compete and when not to, you are in a position to transcend the juvenile questions of who has the bigger biceps, or bubble gum card collection, or brain. And you will be better able to master competition by learning to turn the rules of the game to your advantage when the written ones are against you.

If you can learn to play your own games rather than other people's, you can be a success in most situations, whether you win or lose.

PART I
On Competition

1

WHAT'S GOING ON HERE?
The Many Guises of Competition

In certain arenas of life—politics, work, and sports, for example—competition is constantly visible. It's not hard to spot the urge to win when you're struggling for election, or a raise, or the goal line. In other arenas, however, competitive drives may be so obscured by social conventions and disguises that the casual observer might easily assume they are not operating at all.

That assumption is erroneous: there are virtually *no* areas of human interaction which are free from the urge to win. But because that urge is frequently camouflaged, learning to compete effectively must begin with an understanding of *hidden* competitiveness. We must start by going beneath the polite surfaces of everyday life to the turbulent and complicated core of human interaction.

Ironically, it's often the most ostensibly placid and "competition-free" situations that prove on close inspection to be rife with interpersonal rivalry. Learning to see these situations for what they are rather than for what they seem to be on the surface—learning, in other words, to "read" the signs of hidden competitive urges—can be an important first step in knowing how to act to your best advantage in any given social situation. In this chapter I want to give you an idea of what some of those signs can be.

Imagine, if you will, that you are an invisible guest at a small but distinguished cocktail party. The party is being held in honor of Fred Rojack, an independent contractor who has just landed an important small-business loan from the local bank; the bank offi-cer who arranged the loan, Perry Stiles, is the host.

Now, it's important to know before we study Fred's behavior at the gathering that he comes from an entirely different social background from the other guests, and therefore feels somewhat out of place. The son of a factory foreman, he had only two years of college before he was forced to drop out and go to work. The other guests are, most of them, from Ivy League backgrounds. Moreover, Fred's style of presenting himself is straightforward, unsubtle: he is used to saying what he feels; the Stiles crowd, on the other hand, depends to a great extent on indirection, elegant phrasing, and diplomacy in its pursuit of social status. Flattered that he is being feted by the "Court Street set," Fred still feels a little as if he is not so much on display as on trial. He trusts his own toughness, persistence, and honesty, but the Stiles home is far removed from a construction site, and he is more than a little wor-ried that he will somehow muff the evening.

Fred's first encounter is with Stiles's brother-in-law, a young lawyer named Danny Marchant. Perry seems to beam with frater-nal pride as he introduces the two men.

"You ever have any trouble, any legal problems with the new business, Fred, you go to Danny here. Best damn lawyer in town." His hand rested momentarily on Danny's shoulder.

Fred smiled shyly. Danny, he could see, was another Ivy Lea-guer, and he felt his guard going up already. But, as his host moved on to other introductions, he did his best to be both inter-ested and cordial. Danny took the initiative with him.

"Perry says you're starting your own business, Mr. Rojack. Building materials, is it?"

"Construction," corrected Fred.

"Really?" the younger man said. "Isn't the building business a little slow these days? Interest rates and all?"

"It has been a little slow," Fred admitted. "But your brother-in-law has arranged a loan so we can bid on the development con-tract out in Reseda. He seems confident that—"

"Oh, well, that's different, of course. If Perry thinks we can use more houses, then you're certainly on the right track."

There was a loose laughter in his voice which might have been intended to put Fred at his ease, but didn't. Fred covered by throwing the ball to Danny.

"What kind of legal work do you do?"

"What do you need?"

Fred smiled as graciously as he could manage. "I don't really need a lawyer now. Apparently Mr. Stiles . . . Perry . . . thinks you're top-notch, though."

Danny laughed. "Seems that way to you, does it?" He took a gulp of his drink. "Perry doesn't know a damn thing about me. Humors me is all. Does it all the time. Harvard boy, you know."

He was drunk, and smiling a little too earnestly. Fred was relieved to see that his own glass was empty, for it meant he could slip away to the bar. A few more pleasantries were exchanged, the two men nodded, and Danny wobbled off.

A harmless conversation? Devoid of competitive pressure? Hardly. As you can see in this exchange of strangers, jockeying for position and one-upmanship are already beginning to play a role in the interaction. On the surface, the two men seem simply to be trading inquiries about each other's occupations. In fact, underneath, there is a strong element of nervous reticence on Fred's part and brash defensiveness on Danny's.

Notice how laconic Fred is in his responses, giving out only the meagerest of information about himself: he tells Danny, in fact, nothing that Danny himself does not already know. This is because he is already feeling like a microscopic specimen in this gathering, and is unwilling to give up any more of himself to the investigating parties than he has to. He maintains his edge in the conversation by becoming almost mute; if the lawyer doesn't know anything about my business affairs, he figures, he'll have nothing to use against me.

Danny's tactics are quite different. He is not at all shy about divulging information about himself, or about making observations that might be seen as undiplomatic. His comment about the slowness of the building industry may be seen as a rebuke, a quite unnecessary prod which serves the function of maintaining his edge over Fred. You're building your house on sand, he's suggesting, while I'm on solid ground.

At the same time, Danny's sarcastic comment about Perry reveals something about *why* he is so eager to prove himself a more solid citizen than Fred. Obviously, as a guest in the Stiles house, Danny cannot be outwardly insulting to his host, yet his feeling of rivalry with his brother-in-law is very intense, and he deals with it by resorting to indirection and flippant humor. Simultaneously, he drinks to excess, and spends as little time as possible with Fred: a long, close contact might reveal him to be quite the opposite of the "best damn lawyer in town."

Later we will see how Danny's early life experiences shaped his present behavior. Here it's enough to mention that, since childhood, he has felt extremely jealous of his sister Barbara—now Perry's wife—and that the jealousy in recent years has spilled over into his reactions to Perry himself. His drinking and his sarcasm may be seen, then, as competitive tools: they enable him to keep from getting genuinely involved with the Stiles's other guests, and they serve the added purpose of somewhat embarrassing his host in his own home.

It will be a while before Fred becomes aware of this dynamic in Danny's personality. At this moment, he is being approached by Barbara, and if you look at the way she treats him you can see not only why her own brother resents her so much, but also something about how such seemingly "uncompetitive" behavior as charm and flair can be used to enhance social position.

Barbara Stiles is the epitome of the gracious, bubbling hostess. Dressed in a gown which has obviously been designed less for comfort than for display, she weaves her arm through Fred's with the ease born of long practice, and exhorts him to "mingle" with the others.

"You simply must mingle, Mr. Rojack. My parties are famous for mingling. You wouldn't want me to get a bad name at the Club?"

"Sorry," Fred apologized. "I guess I'm a little bowled over by it all. A lot of new responsibility, you know. I'm still like a cat in his first alley fight."

"Bowled over, Mr. Rojack, how quaint," Barbara replied coolly, ushering him toward a trio which included her husband, a woman in a pantsuit, and a sandy-haired young man Fred had seen at the bank but had not met.

"And so you should be," she continued. "It's a marvelous thing, such an important loan. You should be very proud. But you can't hide your candle, you know. Perry, you're neglecting our guest of honor. Martin and Joan Blakely, this is Mr. Rojack, Perry's latest find. He's going to build houses across the river. Isn't that nice?"

The other banker extended his hand. "Nice to meet you, Mr. Rojack. From what Perry tells me, you may turn Reseda into a gold mine."

"I don't know about that. But we would like to put up some good low-income housing."

"High time, too."

The voice belonged to Joan Blakely, the woman in the pant-suit. It had a cold, piercing quality.

"Yes," Fred agreed. "Reseda has been neglected a long time."

"Because the bankers haven't got the guts—"

"Come on now, Joanie! Don't get on your high horse about the loan situation again."

"Old man Finley's redlining policies ruined my father, and a good many other people besides, and you know it, Martin. He should have left twenty years before he did."

"Well, that's all past history now, Joan." The voice was Perry Stiles's; it was soft, lulling. "The bank has a new policy now, a new management. Fred here is an example of that."

"Really, Joan, you're so one-sided about this thing," Barbara said. "Perry has worked himself into a frazzle putting these small business loans through. We missed out on Juan-les-Pins this year, you know."

"Poor baby," smiled Joan.

"You can laugh," retorted her friend, "but didn't I hear that you and Martin had decided to spend a week at one of those Club Med resorts this summer? Really, Joan. If you must go to the Caribbean, why that way? Who goes to those places anyway? Stockbrokers and secretaries. What will you do there?"

"I'll read, Barbara. I'll write you six postcards a day. If worse comes to worst, I'll talk to Martin."

The jibe broke the developing coolness, and the group, Fred included, chuckled in relief.

You can see in this interchange, however, that rivalry comes in many shades and nuances. Barbara and Joan, who have been social rivals for years, are far more direct and obvious in their bickering than Danny and Perry allow themselves to be. What's interesting to note here are the competitive tools these two women employ. Both are upwardly mobile, status-conscious young matrons, and they use the mildly cutting wit which is accepted humor in their set. But Barbara's smiling haughtiness is not only appropriate to her role as Rising Young Banker's wife; it is a particularly effective tool against Joan, because, unlike most of the party guests, Joan is not a born-and-bred product of Court Street society: she has married in, through Martin. Barbara's caustic remark about the Blakelys' Club Med vacation plans, then, may be seen as a way of putting the interloper in her place. You may have as big a house as we do, Barbara is implying, but at heart you're still a girl from the sticks.

Joan, for her part, even though she is eager to be accepted into the Stiles's group, has a great deal of ambivalence about her new wealth, and as a result often uses guilt-inducing remarks to suggest to Barbara and her crowd that their social consciences are less acute than they might be. But since Joan's father, a merchant, had been ruined by the very bank which her husband Martin now works for, the pleasure she gets out of waving the flag of guilt in front of Barbara is frequently offset by the chagrin she feels at her own compromised position.

So Joan, who seems on the surface less catty and less involved in self-display than Barbara, is actually just as firmly entrenched in competitive maneuvers as her friend. Her very marriage to Martin, in fact, may be seen as a way of retaliating at the forces which ruined her father. By marrying "up" into Court Street, she has been able to partially overcome the feelings of rejection that tormented her as a girl; unconsciously, she married Martin to join a society she knew she had no hope of beating.

Barbara is more blatantly competitive than Joan. Even when she is silent, she is really still playing competitive games. Her flamboyance in dress, for example, is a sign that she is continually out to prove her excellence over others. As hostess, she might be expected to be a bit flamboyant, but she really does not have to dress as ostentatiously as she does, or try to impress Fred with the "specialness" of her parties, or demand that he behave in a way that would glorify her own ego. She does all these things partly to call attention to herself and partly to intimidate Joan—both quite obvious competitive measures.

What of Perry and Martin, the young, up-and-coming bankers? Clearly, in the office they would have to be quite competitive on the job. But is their behavior in this relaxing, "social" atmosphere free of competition?

Not at all. Although Perry may seem the perfect host—friendly, gracious, and eager to involve Fred in the party—his interest in the contractor is anything but altruistic. Nor is his purpose simply to put his guests at their ease. In every social situation he encounters, Perry balances charm with wit, tact with a readiness to listen, in a way that reinforces his image as a thoroughly competent, thoroughly likable fellow. He does this, however, not out of any particular desire to be well-liked, but because he knows that such an image can help him get ahead in business. And since getting ahead is for him, as for his wife, the principal focus of his life, he has made friendliness and charm his stock-in-trade.

The cocktail party should be seen not only as a celebration of Fred's good fortune in securing the loan, but as a public announcement of Perry's latest coup. At the same time, the fact that Perry is "sponsoring" Fred's debut into Court Street society will, he hopes, reflect well on him once Fred becomes a social as well as a business success. Thus Perry's very generosity may be seen as a competitive gesture.

Perry directs that gesture partly to the business community at large, but partly to a particular rival, Martin Blakely. Perry's support of Fred not only increases his overall prestige; it is a mark in his favor against Martin, his longtime "friendly enemy."

Martin, a member of the corporate training program, is spending several years working in each of the different sections of the bank rather than concentrating, as Perry does, on one. It's not surprising that Fred has not met Martin before the party, or that Martin's response to him is relatively straightforward and genial. Since Fred is "Perry's man" (and he knows it), Martin does not waste time at the party, or in the bank, competing for his favors.

Both Martin and Perry come from privileged backgrounds, yet there's a big difference in their approach to competitive success. Perry needs his coups, or "finds" as Barbara calls them. Martin has less of a need to prove himself, and puts in his thirty-five hours a week without worrying about overtime or weekend work. He has actually chosen the corporate training program—rather than a specialty such as loans—because he knows that it will ensure his success: practically everyone who is able to complete the program goes on to become a vice-president, and so his future is set.

In a way, Martin is playing it safe, and this annoys his more industrious friend. The entire party may be seen in a sense as a message from the loan officer to the potential VP: "See, I can take risks and still succeed. You've taken the easy route."

In the Stiles/Blakely rivalry Fred serves as both a major bargaining chip and a pawn. This is not a customary position for him to be in. As a hardworking kid from the wrong side of town, he has been far more accustomed to courting others than being courted himself, and it's clear that, though flattered, Fred is ill at ease.

So far, all of the guests we have met—with the exception of Fred himself—are in one way or another social climbers: to all of them, the advantages of wealth and power are obvious, and to all but Joan, those advantages have been given to them as a birthright.

We have seen how this kind of person, with his or her peculiar approach to social competitiveness, could make a man like Fred Rojack uneasy. Imagine, though, how he would react to quite a different kind of personality. Imagine you are standing at his elbow (still invisible, of course) as he is approached by a trim, bright-eyed woman of about forty.

"I'm Wanda Collins. You're the honored guest, I hear from Danny."

Fred shook her hand. She had an open, eager expression and a grip that wasn't learned in any finishing school. Barbara Stiles's voice, welcoming the newcomer to the circle, betrayed just a hint of envy.

"You should see this one, Mr. Rojack. Up every day at six, jogging. Eight hours at the gallery. Then more jogging. And with a teenager too. I don't know how you do it, darling. You know, Mr. Rojack, she has a Wonder Woman outfit in her closet."

"I'm in training," Wanda explained simply. "The marathon is next month."

"Marathon!" Martin looked shocked. "You're not going to enter that thing, after what Dr. Hartley told you?"

"Beth Hartley has been a Nervous Nelly since the day she was born, and I've been wanting to run a marathon for years. Nobody lives forever, in case you haven't heard."

Fred liked this woman. Not only was she the only person at the gathering who didn't make him feel like an outsider, but she exuded a direct exuberance, uncomplicated by "manners." He was therefore delighted when she stuck an elbow in his ribs and said, "So, guest of honor, what is it we're honoring you for?"

"I've won the Reseda project contract, thanks to a loan from Mr. . . . uh . . . Perry."

"Perry, you sweetheart! Who would have thought a vicious tennis player like you would have a soft spot in his heart for the underprivileged?"

"Underprivileged, my eye," said Martin Blakely. "Damn good business is what it is."

"Of course," admitted Perry. "Land development is always a good investment. Not nearly as speculative as some ventures I might name." He cast a teasing eye at Wanda Collins, and Fred searched in vain for the meaning. "Gallery" could mean "gallery of homes," he supposed.

"You're not in real estate too?" he asked her.

"A marriage made in heaven," quipped Barbara.

"Afraid not," replied Wanda. "Gallery as in art. I own a small shop downtown. I buy things for people like Perry and Barbara."

"And some very nice things they are," chimed in their hostess. "The Stella is simply perfect. As I see my brother has discovered."

Fred's eyes followed hers to where, against a far wall, Danny Marchant was swaying slightly in contemplation of a small, lighted canvas. It looked to Fred like four pale horizontal lines on white.

"Are you in the market for art, Mr. Rojack?" Wanda asked.

"No," Fred replied. "Not yet, anyway. Well, I mean that I don't really know very much about it."

"Excuse us," Wanda said abruptly, taking Fred's elbow to guide him away from the circle. Over her shoulder she laughed, "I think I've found another pigeon." But to him, in a lower voice, she added, "Neither does anybody else. Only none of them will admit it."

Danny turned slightly as they approached. When he spotted Wanda, he uttered a long sigh of mock exasperation.

"Sooo . . . the expert approaches. Tell me, Mr. Kojack, how much would you suppose my dear sister and her husband shelled out to Ms. Collins here for this modern masterpiece? How much do you figure it's worth, I mean?"

"I don't know anything about art."

"Take a guess. Come on, just one guess."

The young lawyer was getting drunker, and Fred was already tired of him. "Fifty dollars," he volunteered.

Danny's eyes looked toward heaven in an expression of resigned despair. He turned to Wanda, but she only touched Fred's arm lightly and shrugged. "He said he didn't know anything about art, Danny."

"Five thousand dollars! That's how much she got for it. And the guy's not even dead yet. Hell, I only paid four thousand for my de Chirico. Shrewd, shrewd . . ."

"The bottom has gone out of the surrealism market, chum. You'd be lucky to get two and a half for the de Chirico now. The minimalists, on the other hand—"

"You and your damn minimalists!" Danny cast a contemptuous glance toward the picture. "Look at that," he said. "If you gave your kid a ruler and a bucket of whitewash, she could do as well as that. I need a refill."

He was off, and it was Wanda's turn to be exasperated. "He's sweet," she said, "but hopeless. He'll never forgive me for charging him less for his picture than I did Perry and Barbara for theirs."

"Must be a strange business."

"Mr. Rojack, you are a master of understatement."

Wanda Collins appeals to us immediately, just as she does to Fred. Enthusiastic, straightforward, and candid, she seems to display exactly that directness which is lacking in most of the Court Street set. Unlike the others at the party, she is little involved in games of one-upmanship or social backbiting. Yet we would be mistaken in calling her uncompetitive. One reason that she does not employ the same catty tools as Barbara is that, as an outside expert (like Fred), she does not really have to. Since she is known in this group as an authority on modern art, she can rely on her own knowledge to give her the aura of prestige which Barbara or Joan must come by more indirectly.

This is an important factor to keep in mind when you are analyzing competitive behavior. Generally speaking, those with true expertise have little need to display it in public; it is those who are most unsure of their social acceptance who frequently overcompensate by lording it over others. Wanda and Fred are both good examples of this principle. It is not that they are inherently less competitive than the rest of the people at the party, but that their competitiveness takes a somewhat different guise.

Notice, too, that for all her self-confidence, Wanda does make a few concessions to the social amenities, and those concessions indicate that, within this group at least, she has learned how to modify her competitive stance to get what she wants. Her off-handed mention that she is about to enter a marathon, her chiding Perry about his supposed concern for the "underprivileged," even her ingratiating manner of confiding to Fred that he is not alone in his ignorance of art—all of these things should be seen as artful, even if unconscious, maneuvers by a person who is extremely flexible in her approach to social gamesmanship and not in the least intimidated by her "betters."

Wanda makes no attempt to climb socially with Barbara and Joan, or to pit herself against their husbands in terms of business acumen. Although she is an extremely successful businesswoman in her own right, she knows when to play the social game to win and when to back off gracefully. She is a person, in other words, who has learned well the lesson that I discussed in the Introduction: if you cannot succeed at another person's game, you must concentrate on what you do best. What Wanda does best is to understand the art market. She sticks to her area of expertise and succeeds.

Because of her confidence, moreover, Wanda can afford to compete in certain areas even when she knows she can't win. Think of her ostensibly casual remark about Perry's tennis playing. On the surface, this may seem a gentle enough poke in the ribs. What lies behind it, though, is a history of unsuccessful competition with Perry on the court, and we should see the remark as further evidence that Wanda knows how and when to play, and when to back off.

Perry Stiles, as you might have surmised from Wanda's allusion, is a terror on the tennis courts. The suaveness and loose charm that he uses to such great effect in business are left behind entirely when he has a racket in his hand. Tennis becomes his way of venting his really aggressive competitive drives, and it enables him to do so in an acceptable social manner.

Realizing this about Perry should help us be aware that the

same person may compete very differently in different situations. This is an important aspect of learning how to compete well in the complex realm of social relations; as we shall see frequently throughout this book, those who succeed most often are those who have access to a wide variety of competitive tools, and can employ them in different ways depending on the nature of the competition and the arena.

It's fairly easy to spot a direct, aggressive competitor. If Fred confronted Perry on a tennis court, he would have no trouble identifying his behavior as clearly, intensely competitive. Confronting the same person at a cocktail party in his honor, Fred cannot be sure what is true friendliness and what are merely the appropriate social amenities; he must, until he gets to know his host and the other guests better, remain somewhat in the dark about their true motivations.

When people are not behaving in an overtly competitive manner, it takes some studying to decipher what is being said to you and why. When you find yourself in a situation such as the one Fred finds himself in at this party, you should endeavor to read constantly between the lines, to sort out the overt messages from the implied ones, to see where the urge to get along drifts subtly into the urge to win.

What does our hypothetical party tableau reveal about the hidden nature of competition? What does it tell us—what does it tell you as the invisible observer at Fred's side—about the many disguises human beings can invent for the urge to be one up on those around them?

I don't pretend that the scene I've described exhausts the possibilities of competitive disguise. The number of ways in which competition can be presented as something else are probably endless. But I do hope that following Fred around the party has given you a few clues about what to look for the next time you are in a similar situation. I hope it has made you aware, for example, that social charm can conceal quite selfish purposes; that cattiness between social peers is seldom simply "bitchy," but rather serves to garner "points" for one party over the other; that flexibility in the social arena is a far better competitive tool than simply standing your ground; and that, when human beings interact with each other, things are seldom what they seem.

Assuming that competition pervades virtually every aspect of our lives, it might be useful to ask yourself a few simple questions the next time you find yourself in such a situation:

1. What is this person really saying?
2. How is it making me feel?
3. Why is he or she saying it to me?
4. How is it making him or her feel?

I don't guarantee that asking those questions will automatically give you full insight into what is going on around you. But being aware of shades of meaning, of the ways in which things are often other than what they seem to be, can be a good start toward identifying the hidden aspects of competition in your own personality and in those of others around you. In order to be able to deal with competition effectively, you must be able to peer through its disguises first. With this as a basis, you can go on to understanding its effects.

I have said that competition is inescapable, and shown how it often makes its appearance in unexpected places. Before looking at some of those places in more detail, I want to discuss why the urge to win seems a constant in the first place. For this, we will have to look at ourselves as human beasts, and see why vying with each other to win may be not only inescapable but absolutely, biologically inevitable.

2

HOW DOES IT BEGIN?
Nature Versus Nurture

Everybody likes to win.

There is something about coming in first, about achieving a victory over a rival, which seems to fulfill a deep need of the human psyche. Accomplishments of many different kinds give human beings satisfaction, but the ones which are most cherished are often those which are carried through in the face of competitive resistance from others.

The medal we honor most is not the one given for a job well done, but the one given for a job done better than some other job. The immense popularity of competitive sports, the attraction of political contests, and the pervasiveness of social "gamesmanship"—such as that evident in the scenario of the last chapter—all bear witness to the importance of competition as a means of enhancing position, pride, and prestige.

Competition can function in many different ways, at times acting as a kind of social glue, at other times severing the most intimate of bonds. It can be blatant or subtle, aggressive or ingratiating, conscious or unconscious. The ways in which we strive to win are almost as varied as human personalities themselves.

Yet we all do strive to win, in one way or another, and that is of central importance. In almost every culture and at every stage of individual development, people seem to have an urge to achieve victory over others. So omnipresent is this condition that we might be justified in relabeling *homo sapiens;* perhaps *homo contendens* would be a better name for us all.

But the fact of widespread competition is easier to identify than it is to give the reasons for its existence. Since the beginning of time, human beings have wrestled with the implications of competition; only more recently, however, have we begun to come up with explanations as to why it seems such a constant factor in human affairs. Many different theories for the motivations of human behavior can be applied to our competitive interactions, but when attempting to understand the pervasiveness of competition in our lives, I have found two theories most useful: the first is that human competitive behavior is an aspect of "human nature," that it is inherited and is therefore innate and relatively fixed; and the second is that such behavior is a result of specific training and education, and is therefore infinitely fluid and malleable. The distinction between these two schools of thought may be seen as a distinction between a focus on *nature* and a focus on *nurture:* a focus on our genes versus a focus on our environment. The "nature-nurture" controversy, in fact, is a constant theme in current discussions of all types of behavior.

Thesis: The "Nature" School

There are very few people today, and virtually no behavioral scientists, who would subscribe completely to the primitivist notion that the human mind at birth is a *tabula rasa,* or blank slate. The French eighteenth-century philosopher Rousseau was probably one of the West's last major thinkers to support that view. Even fewer, however, would support the somewhat older notion of "innate ideas," formulated in ancient Greece by Plato and popularized a century before Rousseau by the English philosopher John Locke. Nearly all modern theorists, in other words, agree that both innate genetic material (*nature*) and learned experience (*nurture*) are crucial components of human development. Where they differ is in the emphasis they put on the one or the other.

Those who take a basically deterministic view of human development say that a child's—indeed, the human race's—essential constitution is fairly well set at birth. Sociobiologists, in fact, have even begun to suggest that there may be specific genes on the chromosomes for such characteristics as aggressiveness and altruism.

The most extreme advocates of this approach are the supporters of the notion that "anatomy is destiny." Individual personality traits, they would say, are determined purely by biological accident. The excessively aggressive competitor acts the way he does because his genes tell him to do so.

Now, few behavioral scientists would support this "total nature" approach, because it's consistent with our training to believe that behavior can be not only understood but modified to some degree. Most of us, therefore, favor the "nurture" approach, even though we may appreciate fully the importance of behavior's genetic origins.

Yet there is a kind of "modified nature" approach which takes as the origin of human competitive behavior not the prenatal period but the very early childhood period. I want to talk about this approach before going on to discuss the "total nurture" theory, which sees "society" as far more important than genes in determining social behavior.

Many behavioral scientists would fall somewhere in this camp. That is, we recognize heredity as a crucial first element in human behavior, but we see the earliest nurturing experiences— those of the home and family—as equal in importance to the genes, and as far more important than "society."

Competitiveness, we may say, is only partially innate in the human being—that is, it is only to a limited extent part of human "nature"—but it makes its presence felt so early in childhood that we are justified in thinking that we all started out, in one form or another, as "winfants." Competition seems to be present almost from the moment of our birth, and indeed, I have observed what I call *unintentional competition,* which may be interpreted as beginning even before birth.

Now, it's hardly obvious that an infant in the womb is already competing with those born, but when you think of the sacrifices of time and attention a pregnant woman must make for the yet unborn child, the notion is not farfetched. Especially toward the end of pregnancy, many women limit their activity and the attention paid their families, for their own health and that of the baby. Such limitation may be entirely justified, but the father or sibling who feels that he or she has to make concessions to the unborn child may feel "aced out" by the prospective family member—and thus may feel already a victim of competition.

Of course, the baby in the womb does not snicker maliciously over this, but in the eyes of the other family members, he or she has already won an initial contest for affection and attention. Thus, even if competitiveness is not genetically determined, it is already a factor in family interaction even before the new little contender takes its first extrauterine breath.

Once the child is born, matters become more clear-cut. An infant's early cries are usually perceived as statements of immediate needs, and for the most part these needs take precedence over the needs of other family members. Thus, the newborn generally comes out ahead, and this sets up a sometimes troublesome pattern: the young one learns to expect instant gratification, while the older family members learn that, in competition with the young one, their needs will usually take second place. We will see later what difficulties that can create in terms of sibling rivalry.

The unintentional competitiveness of the very young child, then, may be seen as the principal example of innate (or at least prenatal) demands being modified by a small social structure—the family. The first few years of life are a time when the infant's natural impulses to survive, to have its needs met and to be gratified, must constantly be balanced against the other family members' needs. This balancing goes on well before the child can possibly be aware of it. Some social scientists—and all committed behaviorists—would say that the importance of balancing needs is therefore proof that "nurture" has already taken precedence over "nature" as the main influence on competitive activity. Whether the child realizes it or not, learning to wait for a feeding while mother attends to another sibling is one of the first competitive lessons.

Antithesis: The "Nurture" School

Those who see learned behavior rather than genetic propensities as central to human development deny that there is such a thing as "natural" competitiveness at all. When the child cries for the mother and she is busy with something else, he is not so much competing for attention as giving simple expression to his dissatisfaction. The competitive element in his crying enters the picture later, when he is old enough to perceive the connection between mother's busyness and his continued feeling of being hungry. At that point he adopts crying not as an instinctual response, but as a tool to get attention.

This happens fairly early in life. By the time children are in their second year of life, in fact, they turn to a phase of intentional competition, and start to demand what they perceive as their rights. The child at this time often learns the use of the possessive adjective "mine," employing it constantly with other toddlers. The tugs-of-war which occur among children in these years are evidence of how conscious the urge to define one's needs against another has become.

By the start of the fourth year, moreover, the nurturing of competition begins in earnest: we actually start to *teach* our children competitive behavior as part of their acculturation process. The games they are taught to play in nursery school (for example, Musical Chairs, Pin the Tail on the Donkey, various races) are full of winners and losers. The songs they sing frequently allude to winning or being good ("Santa Claus Is Coming to Town"). Fairy tales, especially, may involve contests between "good" and "bad," and there is a message in many of them that if they're good they'll win and if they're bad they'll lose.

By kindergarten and first grade it's gotten much more vigorous. My five-year-old son complains that he's not on the same page of his workbook as the other children. He doesn't know whether he's ahead or behind, but the simple fact he is on a different page suggests to him that he's not competing properly. A tremendous double pressure is already building up: to compete or to conform. Later we will see how this affects children in the classroom.

Once children begin learning what educators used to call "the three Rs," the comparisons made are overwhelming. "I'm better than Jeffrey in math but he's better than me in reading" is a common grade school observation. As the teachers start assigning numerical and letter grades, the competition increases. This continues into high school, where the presence of such policies as "tracking" and "A" and "B" classes makes it impossible for the child to draw any conclusion but the officially sanctioned one: Compete!

In school athletics, competitiveness is seen as an absolutely necessary ingredient. It is the "racer's edge" without which no achievement can be made. This can be damaging, for in many academic settings athletic children function as a kind of "in crowd" determining the limits of social acceptability. The nonathletic child may be made to feel incompetent and unpopular as a result.

But the playing field is only the most obvious arena of stiff school competition. By high school, children are competing for everything: sports, grades, artistic ability, even friendships. And they have gotten used to it, particularly if there are siblings they have been competing with from the time they could crawl. Thus—and this is a mixed blessing—it is relatively easy for them to adapt to these new and expanded areas of competition.

The important thing to remember about this, in terms of the significance of the "nurture" theory, is that what our parents tell us, what our schoolmates and teachers do with us, what we pick up at home and in the playgroup and later in the street—all of this is learned rather than innate behavior. I believe that we indeed have a competitive "code" in our chromosomes, but as for the ways in which we compete, the specific tools and attitudes we adopt to survive in a competitive world—all of this is learned rather than inherited.

Parents, as a result, have an enormous effect on the ways their children compete later in life. Many parents enhance their own sense of success or failure through their children; the children, wanting to please them, can easily pick this up. They will, of course, model much of their behavior, including competitive behavior, on that of their parents. Later in life, schools, peer groups, and social organizations serve much the same function as the parents: they can discourage certain kinds of competitive behavior and reward others.

Because the ways in which we compete can be so greatly modified by our social interactions, the most extreme proponents of the "nurture" theory deny a genetic base to competition at all: everything, they say, is learned. Moreover, since some of them see competition as an evil or unhealthy phenomenon, they go on to say that what has been learned can be unlearned. Human beings, they assert, are not inherently competitive; it is only certain "unhealthy" social situations that make them that way, and those situations should be changed.

The political nature of this approach is obvious. Perhaps the most vocal and insistent of the "nurturists" are the socialist critics who identify "Western" or "bourgeois" free-market ideas as the source not only of competition, but of most of the world's other ills. People compete, they say, because it is in the interest of the ruling classes that they do so; were it not for the profit motive. cooperation would overtake competition as a dominant social force, and the abuses of corporate capitalism would end. In a future socialist paradise, we would find that competition, far from being considered natural, would be seen as a relic of an unenlightened age.

What kind of faith can we place in this argument? The socialist critics may be right to observe that competition in the social sphere has frequently favored the interests of small, wealthy groups rather than the society as a whole. But can we conclude from this unfortunate truth that it is only capitalistic societies which support and nurture competitive behavior? I think that the facts speak otherwise.

If we compare Western capitalistic societies with those of other countries around the world, we find that the free-market countries, and the United States in particular, are frequently termed "aggressive" and "competitive." The fact that we must provide many laws in the economic area to control those who attempt to engage in unfair competitive practices is held up as proof that we are more competitive than other people.

Socialist critics, moreover, charge that the free enterprise ethic *promotes* aggressive competition. Some philosophers and sociologists even say that our competitiveness is by now culturally determined: we have developed a society in which everyone is expected to be aggressively competitive, and woe be to those who fail to learn this central social lesson. Too, this competitiveness has spread from the economic sphere to every other aspect of our lives. We find it in the classroom, on the playing field, in the community at large, even in the bedroom.

Without denying that we are a competitive people, I must point out that intense competition is not exclusively a modern Western behavioral syndrome. Although some aspects—perhaps some types—of competition are unique to our contemporary culture, for the most part competitive strivings are shared by all human societies, and have been from the beginning of history. In the most primitive societies, competition within and between tribes for food and shelter is a frequent factor of social interaction—and these are societies in which capitalism has not even been imagined, much less implemented.

Moreover, it's naive to assert that competitive efforts are nonexistent in a socialist setting. Because socialist societies stress a sharing of effort as well as a sharing of products, there's frequently a lack of *material* reward for success within those systems. However, all of the various *psychosocial* rewards, such as respect, recognition, admiration, responsibility, and heightened authority, do accrue to the successful socialist competitor, and these can be every bit as important to him or her as money.

The main difference between competition in a socialist and a capitalist society is that many of the competitive efforts within socialist society are carried out for the good of the state and in a group setting rather than an individual one. This modifies, though it does not eliminate, competitive urges. A group of workers in one factory or collective farm, for example, will compete against other groups of workers in similar settings in order to enhance the general welfare rather than their own personal advantage.

The point I wish to make is that, no matter how a society defines and manages its competitive urges, those urges exist regardless of the social setting. While this is not necessarily an argument for the "naturalness" of those urges, it does suggest that humans, whatever their political persuasions, have not as yet had much luck in "programming" competition out of their behavior. All they have been able to do is to give it a different appearance in different social settings.

This raises a point which may serve to unite the "nature" and the "nurture" schools of thought. Whatever the origin of competitive drives, their ubiquity in human affairs indicates that they do possess not an incidental but a crucial function in the human behavioral mechanism. Whatever their differences in approach, both the geneticists and the environmentalists would agree that any pattern of behavior which is as pervasive as competition must serve a purpose wider than individual needs.

What that purpose might be will, I hope, become clear in the next few pages.

Synthesis: What Use Competition?

Since competition often has negative consequences, we are justified in wondering what benefits accrue to human beings in general from the prevalence of competitive drives.

The answer, I believe, may be found in the field of biology.

Human beings are fond of identifying themselves as very special animals, sharing with the other animals certain structural characteristics and physical needs, but departing radically from them in terms of emotional and mental complexity and creativity. The human psyche, we know, is a uniquely complicated mechanism, one which simply cannot be compared to those of our animal cousins. Evolution can explain only the beginnings of human psychological development, for humans are so far advanced over the other animals as to be rightly judged an entirely different order of creation. Throughout our history, we humans have been ever more successful, to borrow Lord Tennyson's phrase, in "working out the beast" within us.

Is this encouraging picture of human evolution justified? The answer is not clear, but to gain a real understanding of why we humans are universally so eager to win, I think we must look at competition not only historically, but prehistorically as well: that is, we must study our animal ancestors to see how they dealt with winning.

What we find in the animal kingdom is that competition is not only as central as it is among humans, but that it serves a critical biological function as the very hinge of self-preservation.

According to Darwin's *Origin of Species,* every living species has an innate biological drive to survive and to propagate itself. Darwin called this drive the self-preservation instinct. In response to this drive, every living creature strives to attain those basic life supplies necessary for its survival: food, water, shelter, the opportunity to sleep, and so on. But since in nature there is a limited supply or availability of these things, animals must compete among themselves to acquire them. In this competition only the "fittest" survive—and this ensures that, generation after generation, each species will improve in adaptability.

Thus, over time, competition works to the advantage of the species as a whole. Weaker members die, leaving no offspring. Stronger members survive and their genes are passed on to their offspring, improving the overall fitness of the stock.

The relatively recent science of sociobiology attempts to apply Darwinian principles to that all-too-human animal *homo contendens.* Observing that aggression is a constant in human interactions, such writers as Robert Ardrey, Desmond Morris, and Konrad Lorenz have demonstrated that human aggressive impulses may be seen as an inheritance from the animal past, when aggression against members of one's own species served a specific, preservative function.

But is such aggression as useful today as it was in the days when humans first walked the earth?

We no longer live in the fields, after all. We no longer compete directly, as animals do, for the essentials of life. We like to flatter ourselves by thinking that the Law of the Jungle does not apply to our modern human societies. Perhaps, then, we have reached a watershed in the biological interpretation of human competition. For, as society changes the way humans relate to each other, it also changes the functional nature of competition. It may be that, as socially interlocking actors in the complicated drama that is human society, we have indeed "worked out" some of the beast in us, or at least the *usefulness* of our bestial impulses. We may have evolved socially to the point where competitiveness—our ancient animal heritage—no longer serves the purpose it did when we still lived in the trees.

As brute strength gives way to cunning, as purely physical aggression gives way to the subtleties of law and custom, the human beast must find a way to transcend, or at least modify, its past. According to Darwin, all competition is ultimately good, since it serves the long-range improvement of species. But can this really be said about humans?

The most tragic observation of the sociobiological theorists is that human beings may have evolved quite sophisticated forms of social manners with which their primitive impulses are simply incapable of dealing. They liken us to leopards wearing frock coats: the display of social grace is there, but the reality beneath it, to call on Tennyson again, is "nature red in tooth and claw."

Lorenz, for example, feels that the "killer instinct" is *less* controlled in humans than in even the most ferocious of animals. He sees aggression, or the fighting instinct directed against members of the same species, as the outgrowth of the self-preservation instinct, but he believes that technological advancement has caused an overrapid change in the conditions of human life so that aggressive impulses often have destructive results. Thus, although in nature the purpose of aggression is not destruction but survival, humans have distorted it in so many cases that it no longer serves a structural purpose.

Sports activities are seen by Lorenz as an excellent way for humans to channel aggressive drives, just as animals deal aggressively with each other in highly stylized rituals; warfare, however, he calls the result of "misguided militant enthusiasm." He believes that as animals have learned to control their aggressive behavior and deal with it in a functional way for the benefit of their particular species, so, too, can humans learn to deal with aggression and even abolish war. The study of animal behavior, he hopes, will teach us to understand our own aggressive and competitive drives better, so that ultimately we may be able to control them and utilize them for the benefit of all.

Whether this is a vain or realistic hope remains to be seen. What is certain, however, is that the sociobiological approach to the origins of human competitiveness has the advantage of being able to fuse the most positive aspects of both the "nature" and the "nurture" theories. It points out not only what we as humans start out with, but also how far we have yet to go if we are to move beyond "survival of the fittest" to a more complex and humane structure of social interaction.

This "synthetic" approach I've been describing recognizes that certain kinds of competition may be considered "natural," in that they are part of our genetic, suprahistorical heritage: competition for mates, food, territory, shelter, and even "status" may fall into this category. But it also recognizes that the peculiar nurturing of humans gives rise to a panorama of opportunities for competing that could not be imagined by a baboon. Human victors compete for not only material gain, but for such imponderables as power, respect, responsibility, admiration—and all of these may accompany our competitive successes. Similarly, humiliation, degradation, ostracism, or even banishment may, according to the customs of a particular time and place, accompany competitive defeat. This means, therefore, that the opportunities for humans to compete in a destructive, unhealthy manner are infinitely greater than they are in animal societies—for the human being has so many more occasions when he may "lose face" and appear the loser.

Survival may be the name of the competitive game, but so varied have human reactions become to the problems of survival that we need practically a whole new language to investigate the ways in which humans compete when they seem not to be competing at all. Animal gestures, postures, and facial expressions are limited to a small and unwavering repertoire. *Homo contendens,* on the other hand, is the beast with "a thousand faces."

In the following chapter we'll examine some of those faces.

3

THE COMPETITOR'S TOOL BOX:
Styles of Game-Playing

Every living creature competes, but they don't all compete in the same ways. That is one of the things that makes men and women different from animals.

When a baboon, for example, wants the same piece of food as another member of his troop, he has access to a fairly limited range of competitive gestures in order to get his point across. He can bare his teeth, assume a fighting posture, or actually assault his rival physically. There is some difference in style among these choices, but the subtlety is not great, and the competitive message is not hard to read.

Among human beings, on the other hand, there is a significant range of subtlety in any competitive situation, and the styles which humans adopt to best their rivals display an enormous variety and complexity. Yet because we enjoy a much wider repertoire of responses to social situations than the baboons, we suffer the possibility of much greater confusion regarding those responses. The evolution of choice has become like Pandora's box for us: the very range and fluidity of our behavior ensure that crossed signals will be rampant among us.

A great deal has been written in recent years about body language and about how the often unconscious gestures a person makes reveal more about his or her inner feelings than what is actually being said. No one takes a wink or a smile at face value anymore, and every twist and quirk of the human frame is thought to be seething with inner significance. Animals speak with their bodies no less than we do, yet there's no need, for example, for baboons to spend much time poring over guides to simian behavior as a way of understanding their body language. Centuries of breeding have taught them to "read" their own nonverbal language as easily as we humans read words.

But our behavioral repertoire is so much broader that in terms of competition, it's frequently difficult for us to know when we are competing and when we are not. No baboon ever bares its teeth in jest, but humans do this all the time. As a result, it may be, on occasion, nearly impossible to sort out really aggressive behavior from mock-aggressive behavior, or to tell either of these apart from the kind of deviously aggressive behavior which purports to be jocular but is not.

Basic Competitive "Tools"

It would be presumptuous to suppose that one could catalogue all the styles of behavior humans adopt to express their competitive feelings. But we can identify overall patterns, and—allowing for a margin of unpredictability—point to a few recurrent styles in human interaction, in much the same way that primatologists identify threatening, preening, or affectionate behavior in baboons.

The first step is to get some idea of the variety of competitive techniques—I shall call them "tools" here—available to humans; the second is to classify these tools in an organized fashion; and the final step is to use that classification system to identify certain types of competitors.

There are, of course, almost countless types of competitors among humans, just as there are countless types of people in general. But since most people adopt fairly consistent styles of competitive behavior, one of the first things the wise competitor does in any competitive situation is to observe the opponent's techniques: you would not, after all, battle someone wielding a knife in the same way you would oppose someone wielding a pen. Being aware of a particular rival's general approach to competition can thus be a great aid in assessing how to counter his or her moves.

Of the numerous classification systems possible, I have found one to be particularly useful for an understanding of human competitive techniques. This is a four-quadrant matrix which I shall call the Competitor's Tool Box (Figure 1). The tools themselves are divided into two broad categories—*aggressive* and *nonaggressive*. Aggressive tools are those which may cause physical or psychological harm to an opponent; nonaggressive tools are not basically hurtful. The competitor's approach is characterized according to its *direct* versus its *indirect* nature.

In Quadrant I, we find tools used primarily by direct and aggressive (Dag) competitors. In Quadrant II are listed the tools favored by indirect and aggressive (Indag) competitors, while in Quadrant III are those usually employed by direct but nonaggressive (Dinag) competitors. Finally, Quadrant IV outlines the tools used mainly by indirect and nonaggressive (Indinag) types.

Now, in real human interaction it's unlikely you'll find too many people who fit into any of the four quadrants precisely, since human beings are constantly shifting some aspects of their style, "borrowing" competitive tools from quadrants which are not their "own." What makes a person primarily a Dag competitor, for example, is the fact that his competitive endeavors stress the importance of the tools listed in Quadrant I; most of his techniques will come from that quadrant rather than from the others.

All competitors borrow rivals' tools at one time or another—even those whose overall basic style is quite emphatic and distinct. Look, for example, at the character Humphrey Bogart played in such films as *Casablanca, To Have and Have Not, The Big Sleep,* and *The Maltese Falcon.* Most of the time, this character—whether he is called Sam Spade or Philip Marlowe or Mister Rick—is a stoical, sardonic Indinag; with a sly, quiet wit, he generally disarms his opponents by using indirect, nonaggressive tools.

Occasionally, however, the situation calls for this character to borrow tools from another quadrant. Being a generally successful competitor, Bogart is never loath to do so. In *To Have and Have Not,* for example, when he needs desperately to get information from a Gestapo lackey, he resorts to the Dagish tool of physical violence and pistol-whips the man into talking. And in *The Big Sleep,* as Philip Marlowe, he adopts the Indagish tool of cunning and deceit by impersonating a bookworm in order to break through the defensiveness of a bookstore operator who has the information he needs. In both cases, an essentially Indinagish competitor improves his chances of getting what he wants by borrowing the tools of others.

THE COMPETITOR'S TOOL BOX

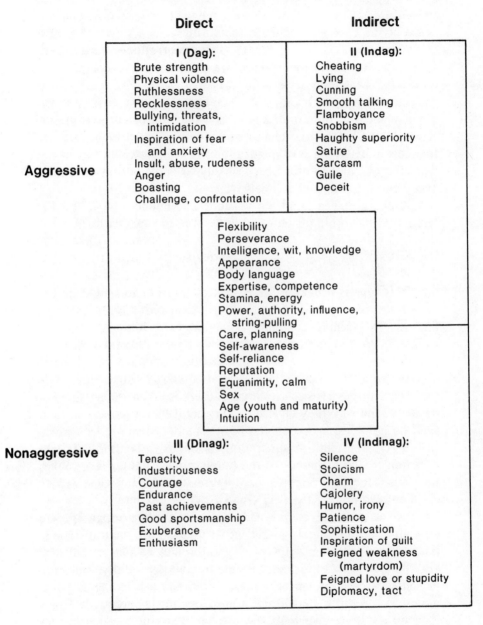

Direct   **Indirect**

Aggressive

I (Dag):
Brute strength
Physical violence
Ruthlessness
Recklessness
Bullying, threats,
   intimidation
Inspiration of fear
   and anxiety
Insult, abuse, rudeness
Anger
Boasting
Challenge, confrontation

II (Indag):
Cheating
Lying
Cunning
Smooth talking
Flamboyance
Snobbism
Haughty superiority
Satire
Sarcasm
Guile
Deceit

Flexibility
Perseverance
Intelligence, wit, knowledge
Appearance
Body language
Expertise, competence
Stamina, energy
Power, authority, influence,
   string-pulling
Care, planning
Self-awareness
Self-reliance
Reputation
Equanimity, calm
Sex
Age (youth and maturity)
Intuition

Nonaggressive

III (Dinag):
Tenacity
Industriousness
Courage
Endurance
Past achievements
Good sportsmanship
Exuberance
Enthusiasm

IV (Indinag):
Silence
Stoicism
Charm
Cajolery
Humor, irony
Patience
Sophistication
Inspiration of guilt
Feigned weakness
   (martyrdom)
Feigned love or stupidity
Diplomacy, tact

Figure 1

Now, certain competitive tools are not confined to any one style; they can be used by all four types of competitors, and because of the existence of these tools, it's necessary to add a fifth classification box to our diagram. This "central box" (see Figure 1) enumerates those tools which are available to all competitors, no matter what their style—and it is the use of *these* tools which generally swings the balance between competitive success and failure. The more of the center box tools which you can utilize, in other words, the better your chances of winning. The person who uses the tools in his or her own quadrant exclusively, without borrowing from the common center box, is likely to end up with an unbalanced and unsuccessful competitive style.

Keeping this in mind, let's take a closer look now at the different styles, defining each quadrant of the tool box in turn.

I: The Direct, Aggressive Competitor (Dag)

This type is probably the easiest of the four to spot. Dag behavior is closest in manner to the uncomplicated, direct rivalry we find in the animal kingdom; a majority of humans, however trained in social conventions, avoid Dag behavior in favor of more subtle varieties of competitive interaction.

We've all run across Dagish people, and although their style may sometimes strike us as abrasive, there is a heartening simplicity about the way they choose to play competitive games. In fact, their no-nonsense approach can be strangely charming. In a world so full of bared teeth masquerading as smiles, it is often a delight to watch the performance of the tough, honest fighter who makes no excuses for his straightforward aggression. John Wayne was an excellent example of the Dag Good Guy.

At its worst, of course, Dag behavior can be appalling. We may all admire a direct, go-getting attitude, but if that attitude is linked to an obsession with winning and a lack of concern for others, the Dag competitor can become a downright Bully, and even in some cases a sociopathic personality. Since winning is paramount to the Bully, he will use almost any tool to ensure it. Common direct aggressive tools include brute strength, physical violence, threats, intimidation, insult, and anger. In the extreme, in other words, directly aggressive competition is antisocial, and tends to create a closed, nervously competitive atmosphere rather than the open, fluid one that might be expected in the presence of such direct people. Who wants to sail with Melville's Captain Ahab or make the Grand Tour with Attila the Hun?

What can be done about the ruthless, bullying type of competitor? Fortunately, this type of person often has a fatal flaw. So intent is he on winning that he frequently forges ahead blindly without considering strategy, and this can lead to his undoing. He may become so rigid and inflexible that his inability to change strategies when necessary dooms him to failure. The wrestler, for example, who leaps viciously and blindly for his opponent's head the minute the bell sounds may well find himself flat on his back shortly thereafter. The ruthlessly Dagish competitor often suffers from a lack of feedback as to how well he is doing, and his zeal to win frequently proves ineffective against a strategy of judicious caution.

Not all Dags are ruthless. Many of them, though no less eager than the Bully to win, are much more discriminating about *how* they win. Dagish competitors of this sort can be very exciting rivals, calling up the best in their opponents as well as in themselves because they are eager to win without being obsessed by it, and because they display a sheer, wild recklessness without that ruthless edge. We have all cheered as Errol Flynn picked up his enemy's sword and gave it back to him.

I refer to this kind of Dag as the Buccaneer. Buccaneers are challenging, reckless, and energetic—sometimes almost manic in their drive. The Buccaneers' tools include boasting, displays of courage, and confrontation, but they also may borrow enthusiasm and endurance from the nonaggressive tool box at times. They want to win and they let everyone know it, but—unlike Bullies—they seldom resort to underhanded methods to ensure their success. And since they play the game fairly, they are a good deal more enjoyable to compete with than the more extreme Dag types.

What these two different Dag types share is a commitment to victory and a willingness to acknowledge that commitment publicly. Because of their zeal for winning, they are extremely difficult to stop. But because of their openness about their goals, they are quite easy to identify, and this makes them easier to confront than indirect types.

II: The Indirect, Aggressive Competitor (Indag)

Indag competitors are not so easy to spot. That is, it is not so easy to see that they are competing, because they use various indirect tools to disguise how important winning is to them—although they may be every bit as aggressive and concerned with victory as the Dag people.

Many Indag competitors adopt a careless, unconcerned attitude about their attempts to win, and this often serves, paradoxically, as a key to their success. You know that the Bully is out to get you, but you're not always sure with indirectly aggressive people, and so competing successfully with them takes a good deal of perceptiveness.

One of the most common Indag competitors is the character I call the Showman. He has perfected the flamboyant, devil-may-care approach so well that it frequently appears he is not competing at all. "It's only a game" becomes a kind of watchword for these people: winning, it would seem, is less important to them than playing the game with flair. So deftly do they manipulate the play, however, that they often seem to be winners even when they lose. Jack Benny and Groucho Marx were prime examples of Showmen. They used Indagish tools such as charm, cajolery, humor, irony, and even feigned stupidity to overcome their opponents.

I used to play tennis with a man called George. We were about equally matched, but George was a consummate Showman. He would lunge for the ball madly even when it was within easy reach and would keep up a constant patter all during the game, which had the dual effect of making him seem preoccupied and of unnerving me. At the end of the game, he would invariably leap the net to congratulate me, managing even then to make it appear that he had played the better game. He was the classic Good Sport, but his high spirits had an ulterior, indirectly aggressive motive: they were designed to make me feel as if I were overdoing things by taking the game seriously. In fact, it was George who was in deadly earnest about winning.

Barbara Stiles, whom we met in Chapter 1, is another example of the Showman type of personality. She used a variety of indirectly aggressive tools to get one up on her rival, Joan Blakely.

These included flamboyance in dress, a haughty superiority, sarcasm, and a generally snobbish tone which was meant to convey to all present that she was really above it all.

The indirect and aggressive tools employed by the Showman type are a grab bag of harmless-looking but quite deadly devices. If the Dag person is fond of bludgeoning an opponent into submission, the Indag type prefers to knife his rival (quietly) in the back, while the onlookers believe he is actually giving his victim a pat of encouragement. Satire, cunning, feigned stupidity, and even lying are all commonly employed by this type of competitor.

Often, when you are pitted against an Indag, you hardly know you're playing the game before you've lost. This is especially so in the case of the Cheat, an Indag competitor whose zeal for winning allows him to completely subvert the rules of the game in his drive to finish first. Like the Bully, the Cheat considers victory more important than the way the game is played, and will often stop at nothing to ensure a win. Indeed, Bullies who feel they are losing will often turn to indirectly aggressive tools such as cheating as a means of achieving victory. The Cheat consistently uses lying, cunning, and deceit. This is the main competitive style of spies and saboteurs. Dealing with the Cheat is like being taken to Watergate for dinner by the Plumbers.

What can you do against an Indag? Obviously, competing against an indirectly aggressive person is trickier than competing against a directly aggressive one, and you should therefore be on the lookout, whenever you're confronted with a Showman or a Cheat, for signs that he or she is playing to win precisely by appearing *not* to care. Whenever you hear a rival say something like "It's only a game after all," be on your guard. The strategy is that *you* should consider it only a game so *he* can walk off with the prize!

Be especially wary of the witty, good-natured competitor à la Bob Hope. Humor, a nonaggressive tool, is frequently employed by Indag competitors—who are basically aggressive—as a way of throwing opponents off the scent. While a balanced appreciation for the humor of a situation is almost always an asset, you don't want to be in the position of smiling your way into last place. And that is just where the Indag—be he Showman or Cheat—wants you to be.

III: The Direct, Nonaggressive Competitor (Dinag)

The third type of competitor, the direct but nonaggressive person, is a very difficult kind of opponent to beat—even though such people often seem low-key, even meek, in their dealings with other people. The secret to the Dinag's success is tenacity. This type has an enormous ability to see an issue through to its conclusion, a high degree of endurance, and a high tolerance for disappointment. More than any other type, they especially insist on playing the game by their own rules, using their own Dinagish tools. This enables them to keep trying long after their more impatient rivals have been discouraged. These characteristics give them a stable, forceful attitude, and for that reason I refer to the Dinag as the Bulldog type. The difference between Indag and Dinag competitors is that while the Dinag is nonaggressive and does not try to harm his rivals, he admits that he is openly competitive; the Indag will deny that he is competing while he tries to harm you. Churchill, Gandhi, and FDR all were direct nonaggressive competitors with clearly stated goals of winning which they pursued doggedly.

Fred Rojack (see Chapter 1) is a good example of this Bulldog type. He is not flashy or flamboyant. His use of irony and wit is limited. He does not think of himself as better than other people, and so he has no recourse to Barbara's attitude of superiority. Moreover, he has spent years in ostensibly unrewarding labor to advance himself; not his flair, but his steadiness, has finally paid off. Interestingly enough, Wanda Collins, to whom he is attracted, is also a Dinag who displays many of these same characteristics.

Bulldog types are characterized often by a willingness to defer victory to the future, and this is a strong point in their favor as long-range competitors. The Bulldog takes hold of a competitive situation and, no matter how severely he or she is buffeted by fortune thereafter, retains a grip on it until all other rivals fall away. The perseverance, industry, and endurance of the Dinag allows him to win wars even when he has lost all but the last battle. Unlike the Bully, who is also direct, the Bulldog does not need the constant reassurance of success to keep going. Faced with a setback, the Bully is likely to fly into a rage or perhaps borrow some tools from other quadrants (frequently cheating); the Bulldog in the same situation will only dig in his heels all the harder.

It's easy to see, therefore, how difficult it is to compete successfully against a Dinag once he or she has set sights on a goal. I remember a classmate of mine many years ago who was a steady, if uninspired, student. Roger was in competition with Jeff for the school prize in biology with its accompanying scholarship. It was generally assumed that Jeff would win it because he was active in class and displayed a general enthusiasm for the subject that Roger, a sober young man, just didn't have at his disposal.

The prize was awarded, however, not on the basis of class performance, but on the basis of a term project. In this project, which demanded weeks of patient labor, Roger showed his real mettle. Jeff threw together a clever but unpolished experiment in the last few days before the deadline—something which the conscientious Roger could never have done—but it was no match for Roger's winning entry, on which he had worked, without reward, all term.

Competing against a Bulldog, then, requires an extra level of concentration, dedication, and stamina. Aggressive measures, even Indagish tricks, will do very little to dislodge a Bulldog rival.

If what you are competing for demands resourcefulness rather than tenacity, wit or inventiveness rather than hard labor, then Bulldog tactics may be insufficient: Dinag persons are usually notoriously short on surprise moves. The cartoon character Charlie Brown, for example, is a Bulldog who is continually bested by Lucy's Indagish behavior. If the competitive event you are entering is a test of innovation or quick-wittedness, you stand some chance of defeating a Bulldog by employing Indag tools. But if the event is a test of perseverance and industriousness, you will stand about as much chance of winning as the hare did against the tortoise.

IV: The Indirect, Nonaggressive Competitor (Indinag)

The fourth style of competitor is probably the trickiest of all to deal with. Indinags use some of the same kinds of competitive tools as their fellow indirect competitors, the Indags, but because they employ those tools in an elusive and nonaggressive manner it's much more difficult to identify them as competitive types. Indinags, although they seem the *least* competitive of all types, actually have only adopted more circuitous strategies to get what the others strive for more obviously. They are for that reason very difficult rivals to beat. Woody Allen is a prime example of the Indinag competitor. In all his early films he presents himself as a humorous, frequently helpless competitor who is apologetic when he wins. He uses irony, stoicism, and feigned weakness or stupidity very well. It's interesting to note that in *Manhattan,* one of his later films, he has evolved into a Dinag. As a more mature artist, he is able now to be direct even though his basic style still remains nonaggressive.

Indinag people may be stoical or histrionic, friendly or shy. They may use an enormous repertoire of indirectly nonaggressive tools to get what they want, but one element generally links all their techniques: on the surface they do not appear to be using competitive techniques at all. That, of course, is why they are so hard to pin down. As Lucy Ricardo in the popular TV series "I Love Lucy," Lucille Ball was the classic Indinag—so seemingly inept that her opponents became sympathetic and were caught off guard, going down in defeat before they realized it.

Perry Stiles, one of the characters we met in Chapter 1, displays the traits of one common Indinag type, the Charmer. Perry, as we've observed, expertly plays the part of the perfect host. He is suave, solicitous of his guests, and good at getting them to talk about themselves. At the same time he is an accomplished conversationalist himself, with a flair for the mild barb and the bon mot.

Although his talent for putting people at their ease shows to good advantage at his cocktail party, it's important to note that his skills as a host have also served him well in his business dealings at the bank. In fact, it is precisely because of those skills that he has become a respected loan officer.

This pattern is common in the business world. Indinag behavior is frequently applauded there in ways that directly aggressive behavior never is, since the person who can charm clients into signing lucrative contracts is far more highly regarded by his or her peers than the person who resorts to bribery or intimidation. Although the financial effect may be the same in the end, the Indinag victory is almost universally more admired because of its finesse.

When I was in college, I once tried to sell encyclopedias door to door. After my first full day of having doors closed in my face, I trudged home dejectedly, wondering what had gone wrong. I was met by my uncle, a salesman, who asked me what had happened.

"Nothing," I said. "It was lousy."

"Did you tell them you were working your way through college?" he asked.

"No," I replied. "I thought I was selling books, not hearts and flowers."

My uncle laughed, and then told me something I've never forgotten: "No matter what the product, the successful salesman is really always selling the same thing—himself." This is a lesson all Indinag people seem to know by heart. Perry Stiles understands it clearly, for he has made his own graciousness the principal tool in his competitive arsenal. He does not *need* to be aggressive in business; as a Charmer, he accomplishes much more with sweetness.

Not that he is above borrowing more injurious tools if it will serve his purpose. Indinags are not to be confused with Dinagish Nice Guys. They can effectively employ stony silence, cajolery, and even guilt-inducing tactics if they see those techniques as more appropriate than charm in a given situation. The guilt-provoking person is actually an indirect, nonaggressive competitor. The competitor who assumes the role of the Martyr or the Poor Kid is also an Indinag. What is common to each of these types is that they instill a sense of pity or guilty uneasiness in their opponents in order to conceal the fact that they are competing, and this frequently causes their rivals to ease up on their own competitive efforts.

Perry is not averse to employing even blatantly aggressive competitive tools in certain circumstances. When he plays tennis, for example, unless he is wooing a client across the net, he drops the Charmer stance, borrows techniques from Quadrant I, and plays in a direct, hard-hitting manner. Thus, in one situation he functions as a Indinag and in another as a Dag.

Assessing Competitive Behavior

I have sketched here only a few possible types for each of the four main competitive styles: I certainly am not suggesting that all people are either Bullies, or Bulldogs, or Charmers. Not only does everyone occasionally borrow tools from one style or another, but within each style there are nuances of behavior that are far more complex than my brief descriptions would indicate. This is why it is vital to have at your disposal a method of assessing your competitors that allows you to judge the ways in which your rivals adopt different tools to meet the exigencies of different situations. The better you become at identifying the various modalities of competition, the quicker you will be able to say, "Ah, there's an Indag playing the Bully," or "There's a Bulldog type utilizing flamboyance."

The way I would suggest you do this is simply to use the Competitor's Tool Box in Figure 1 as a guide to constructing a kind of personality profile of your competitor. First, look closely at the ways in which the person competes. Then list, on a piece of paper, all the tools you can identify that he or she commonly employs. By comparing that list with those in the Competitor's Tool Box, you should find that the person's major tools are "clustered" primarily in one of the quadrants and in the center box. This will tell you not only what kind of competitor you are dealing with, but also—if there is a balance between center-box and quadrant tools—whether he or she is likely to enjoy a high degree of success.

If, for example, you have listed such tools as silence, feigned stupidity, irony, flexibility, wit, and string-pulling, you can be pretty sure you're dealing with a basically Indinag person who, because he utilizes a balance of quadrant and center-box tools, is probably good at winning. If you list ruthlessness, bullying, tenacity, cunning, and cheating, you're dealing with a Dag who borrows from the other boxes, but unwisely—he does not balance his style with the center-box qualities and you shouldn't expect such a person to be very successful in the long run.

Constructing this kind of personality profile of your rivals, although it will not ensure your success against them, will at least give you some notion of the rules they play by—and thus of what stance you yourself should adopt to compete with them. Constructing a similar profile of your particular competitive style should also give you a better idea of your own strengths and weaknesses.

Remember, too, that because human beings have such a wide repertoire to draw from, and because today's successful tool may prove quite useless tomorrow, the top competitors are generally those who have learned to adapt to changing situations and to borrow different tools as circumstances dictate. They rarely rely solely on the tools of one quadrant. The more resourcefulness you are able to bring to your own competitive style, the better you can deal with a wide range of unpredictable situations.

Appropriate strategies for dealing with competition are, in short, far more complicated than any four- or five-box grid could indicate.

Situational Variables

I want to close this chapter now by mentioning two major outside influences governing competitive behavior. I call these situational variables (see Figure 2). To adequately assess the nature of competition in any given situation, it's necessary to know not only the competitive style of the people involved and the tools they are likely to employ, but also something of the specific situation in which they find themselves. Situation is seldom incidental to behavior; in most cases, it is an important and even determining factor of the successful competitor's approach. (Perry Stiles, you will recall, competed in a quite different manner on the tennis court and at his cocktail party.)

There are two major situational variables which impinge on most competitive situations. The first involves two questions: 1) What is the goal of the competition? Are there many possible winners or only one winner? and 2) Do the competitors know each other? I divide goals into three types: fixed (there can be many winners), semifixed (the number of winners is limited), and unfixed (the best one wins). I also divide competitors into two types: those who are known to each other, and those who belong to a large anonymous field.

These variables have a significant effect on the intensity of the competition and the degree of stress and anxiety experienced by the competitors. In cases where many people are trying to achieve the same fixed level of achievement—such as winning a Scout Merit Badge or passing a licensing test of some sort—there is a low level of interpersonal rivalry, since it is not necessary to beat someone else out for the honor. Everyone who meets the fixed standards can win. The competitive edge may be further softened in these situations because your fellow competitors are frequently known to you. Unknown competitors usually evoke greater anxiety

SITUATIONAL VARIABLES

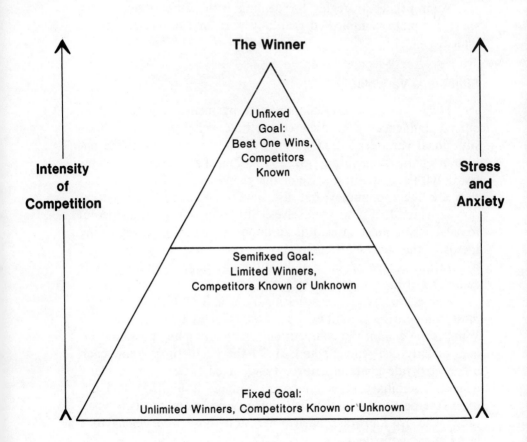

Figure 2

and stress because we tend to magnify our opponents' strengths when we are in a poor position to realistically assess their weaknesses.

In cases where you are striving for a semifixed, limited-winner goal along with a number of other unknown rivals—as in acceptance into college or graduate school—your sense of competitive fervor may increase. This is unlikely to have an effect on the outcome, however, because whether or not your anxiety increases, there is a good possibility of winning if you meet the desired standard. I call this a semifixed goal because once you reach the acceptable standard, you are still measured against the other applicants in order to be a winner.

In situations in which only the best contestant wins, with no fixed goal (winning an athletic race or an art or music competition, for example), rivalry is bound to be more intense than it is in situations where there can be many winners. In these instances, even friends can become temporary enemies. Where the goal is, quite simply, to beat everybody else, interpersonal antagonism, stress, and anxiety are the most intense—and this is so no matter what types of people are competing.

In these "best-one-wins" contests you are most likely to be successful if you are able to adjust your style to meet the demands of the situation. This may entail borrowing tools from other quadrants in order to meet certain exigencies. It certainly demands the use of an array of center-box tools such as flexibility, competence, and perseverance. In these situations, you almost always know your opponents, so you have an opportunity to adjust your own methods after making a realistic appraisal of your competition. If, in spite of your best efforts, you are still losing, this suggests that you should consider revising or adjusting your style (including changing to different tools). You might also increase the intensity of your competitive efforts if possible, or perhaps stop competing in this area altogether and switch to a different competitive arena.

The second major situational variable to be considered is whether the competition takes place on a narrow individual scale or on a wider group scale. People compete quite differently when they have an audience than when they do not, and therefore it's helpful to know, when analyzing competition, to what extent individual effort may be fused with, or confused with, a more general group or team effort.

Obviously, in a world of multiple allegiances such as ours, very little activity can be thought of as purely individual, and for that reason *microcompetition* (individual competitive effort) frequently merges into *macrocompetition* (group or team competitive effort) even in cases where the competitor is not a clear member of a group. As soon as even two people join forces in competition—bridge partners, for example—macrocompetition has entered the equation, and with it a host of concerns not present in microcompetition: Will my partner think I am worthy of his or her partnership? Will my partner help or hinder me? Will my opposition respect me more or less by virtue of my competitive group? And so on.

Another parameter of macrocompetition is the effect it has on individual competitive efforts. For instance, groups in which each member is dependent on the other members for the accomplishment of a designated task (such as a construction crew)—what behavioral scientists call a positive interdependency group—enhance the individual's sense of well-being and self-esteem while decreasing his competitiveness with the other group members. Groups in which each member is directly competing with every other member and can frequently get ahead only at the expense of the others (such as life insurance or real estate salespeople vying for commissions in the same office) constitute what behavioral scientists call a negative interdependency group. These tend to intensify microcompetition and diminish one's sense of self-worth and well-being. As a situational variable, the specific type of group setting you find yourself in will necessitate adjustments in your competitive style if you are to be successful.

AUTOCOMPS:
Competing with Yourself

All the styles of competitors I have discussed up to now compete with each other. Whatever the goal, whatever the nature of the competitive arena, whatever tools are employed, interpersonal rivalry is a dominant feature of their competitive activity. Yet many of us reserve our most intense competitive efforts for ourselves; some of us, indeed, find it all but impossible to compete with anyone *but* ourselves. In this case the protagonist and the rival are one and the same person. I call these competitive situations *autocomps.*

Naturally, the tools one uses on behalf of or against oneself differ somewhat from those employed in efforts to best an external opponent. Few of us are likely to employ direct aggressive methods against ourselves: the notion of punching yourself in the nose as a way of coming out ahead makes little sense either physically or psychologically.

Yet a self-competing person, or autocomper, may employ almost any technique in order to achieve his or her goal. Like people who compete primarily with others, those who compete mainly with themselves may do so, without realizing it, in an indirect or direct manner, in an aggressive or a nonaggressive way.

When I was a child, I never considered myself a very competitive person. Certainly—as demonstrated in the incident down at the creek—my early attempts at athletic competition were not very successful. As a result, I compensated by turning to more cerebral pursuits, concentrating on getting good grades in school. I was obviously competing, but it did not feel the same as overt physical competition.

By the time I got into medical school, I had become quite proficient in intellectual competition, although I continued to view myself as basically less competitive than my more athletic friends. Sports in the United States are so obviously and directly competitive that it was easy for me to delude myself into thinking that my intellectual activity was free of competitive drives. I had convinced myself that intellectual striving had little to do with winning: in the life of the mind, there are no winners or losers, only Truth.

The sports I did engage in were seldom "combat" or team sports. I jogged, I went skiing, I sailed. The sole nod I made to the Urge to Win was that, toward the end of my residency, I took up tennis. (Even on the courts, however, I kept a low profile as a competitor. After playing the game for a couple of years, it became painfully evident that tennis frequently came between "happily married" couples—and indeed, my own marriage a few times drifted into stormy water because my wife and I were beginning, as each other's main tennis partners, to think of winning, rather than enjoyment, as the goal of the game. In addition, our levels of skill were not parallel. Luckily, we were able to separate other aspects of our personal life from our tennis and thus solve the tennis problem by coming to an agreement: winning, we decided, must never get in the way of togetherness or the fun of the game. If it did, we would stop playing.)

Other than tennis, most of my athletic endeavors were noncompetitive. As I started becoming interested in the psychological aspects of competition, I realized that I wasn't alone in preferring noncompetitive sports. In fact, as I began formulating my thoughts for this book, I was repeatedly confronted with people who told me that they were basically not very competitive. Yet as I observed their styles and listened to what they were saying, I realized that, like me, they *were* competitive—but not obviously so. What's more, I saw that many of them were involved in the same kinds of athletic activities as I was, namely those in which you don't need anyone other than yourself to compete with.

If there were so many of us "noncompetitive competitors" around, maybe we weren't freaks after all. Maybe we illustrated a pattern. The more I studied the behavior and life-styles of my fellow "noncompetitors" the more I realized that we shared a common quality. We did not need—or did not want—to measure our prowess against the world. We were content to measure it against an internal standard, and to act, therefore, as our own judges and cheering squads. I decided to call such self-competing individuals "autocompers."

An autocomp—a pattern of competition which substitutes an internal for an external standard of appraisal, and in which the competitor is actually pitted against himself or herself—can serve a number of purposes. Three, however, stand out:

1. It may be used as a way of enhancing self-esteem.
2. It may be used as a way of avoiding direct interpersonal competition.
3. It may be used as practice or training, prior to interpersonal competition.

Let's examine each of these in turn.

Enhancing Self-Esteem

If we accept the basic premise that the origins of our competitive drives are tied to our primitive instincts for self-preservation and survival, and that these urges have evolved in modern humans to the point where our ego development and psychological well-being are in part predicated on our ability to compete sucessfully, then we can see why autocomps are a necessary aspect of our behavior.

Successful ego development demands that each of us find some area in which he or she can excel. Traditionally, the world of sports provides the earliest competitive area, but since not everyone is naturally athletic, it's obvious that only a few of us will ever be able to come out as winners in sports. The rest of us, then, have to devise alternative areas of excellence if we are to maintain our early sense of self-esteem. For, in spite of all our talk about "losing gracefully" and developing "good sportsmanship," the fact is that it doesn't feel very good to lose.

The way I met this problem was to channel my energies into schoolwork, and in that I was generally successful. Other children frequently take up hobbies: they strive to put together a collection of the "best" or the "most" or the "biggest" of a particular item.

Still others turn to exotic sports, such as polo or jai alai, in which their peers cannot easily compete with them. But the majority of nonathletic children develop interests which are tangential to, rather than in direct competition with, those of their peer group. They take up hobbies, for example, in which there need be no winning or losing, in which excellence is not measured by reference to how someone else is doing. In other words, they take up autocomps.

Autocomps are an exceptionally beneficial way for the nonathletic child to overcome his or her feelings of worthlessness or isolation. If I am engaged principally in autocomps, I can set a goal without telling anybody about it. I can reach it or miss it, and nobody will be critical but myself and my own conscience. I can change my goal each day and continue to feel better about myself every time I meet a new goal. If on a particular day I don't work hard enough or fail to meet my goal, I don't have to answer to anybody but myself. Autocomps therefore can be a lot less threatening and anxiety-provoking than competition with others. They are a way of ensuring self-esteem which does not run the risk of invidious comparison.

Of course, nonathletic children are not the only ones who engage in autocomps, but the reasons for doing so are usually different for those who are athletically inclined. In some cases this form of competition can become counterproductive. Sometimes a person engages in autocomps exclusively—not for the pleasure of developing self-esteem, but simply to *avoid* losing.

Avoiding Competition

Hobbies, as I've just mentioned, often function as channels for competitive energies in children who are for one reason or another wary of direct competition. I recall a childhood friend who, as a way of directing attention away from his poor athletic abilities and awkwardness with girls, spent hours each day working on a large and eventually quite impressive baseball card collection. Carl was shy and often the butt of the other children's humor, but when he began to devote himself to his collection he rapidly became known in the neighborhood as an "authority" on trading cards. As a result (even though he himself may not have been capable of fielding a grounder), he was constantly sought out to settle disputes about batting averages, club affiliations, and RBI statistics. He had succeeded in diverting his energies into something he could do well. And in mastering an autocomp, he simultaneously avoided unpleasant comparisons on the playing field and the dance floor.

Such re-direction of energies is especially common in cases of success-fearing and failure-fearing personalities. Persons with a success-fearing personality may be afraid to compete because, as the name implies, they are afraid to win: afraid to invoke the wrath of a bested opponent, or to expose themselves to the scrutiny that winners often elicit. Such types frequently turn to autocomps as an alternative to dealing with their need for self-validation. But, depending on the severity of their problem, just as they undermine themselves in interpersonal competitive situations, they may also sabotage their own self-competitive efforts when they are close to exceeding a previous goal. (They would especially do this in situations where others became aware of their autocomps, for their greatest difficulty is being successful in the eyes of others.)

The failure-fearing personality may also turn to autocomps as an alternative to interpersonal competition, since a principal advantage of autocomps over interpersonal contests is that in them failure and success are not easily measured from the outside. This, I think, was the operative principle with my friend Carl. He had actually set very high goals for himself (I remember his confiding to me once that he was planning to collect "every New York Yankee ever printed"), but only he was aware of this. Therefore, even if he didn't achieve his goals, nobody would know and he could save face among his peers.

To some extent, you don't have to feel like a loser if you lose an autocomp. If you fail to reach your goal, you have limitless opportunities to try again without fear of censure if you fail. This in itself makes autocomps attractive to those who are competitively uncertain of themselves. Some people who have a need to punish themselves use autocomps (as well as other types of competition) to set themselves up to fail: by choosing unattainable goals in a self-destructive way, these masochistic individuals prove that they are as "bad" as they fear they are.

Autocomps as Practice

Not everybody who engages in autocomps does so for negative or compensatory reasons. Many people who are directly and aggressively competitive are also quite well-versed in autocomps. In some cases, this is because they have used autocomps earlier in their lives to *prepare* for the interpersonal type of competition at which they excel now. In addition, once a person is acknowledged as a successful competitor, he or she will often still use autocomps for practice, as a means of increasing skill and confidence even more. Obviously, the use of an autocomp in this way differs from its use as a means of avoiding competition. The marathon runner, for example, who drives himself or herself to do five, then ten, then fifteen miles at a single clip in training for the Boston or New York marathon is practicing an autocomp, to be sure—but its ultimate function is to enable the runner to compete better in the public, interpersonal race.

Even the most aggressive and direct competitors are not born that way. Success in this type of competition often requires years of practice and prior training, and the person who seems so confident today in his or her competitive endeavors may well have passed through difficult periods when winning came anything but easily. In those periods, autocomps very likely served as self-validation, just as they do on a regular basis for people who are not successful in interpersonal competition.

Autocomps, like other forms of competition, are so much a part of the fabric of contemporary society that we frequently fail to recognize them. A distinct social milieu has grown up around such "noncompetitive" athletic activities as jogging, yoga, and marathon running, and in some cases that milieu dictates far more about a person's performance than requirements of health or endurance. It has become chic to jog, to ski, to play tennis—and people engage in these sports with a single-minded devotion *whether or not they are any good at them.* To say that you are "improving" your backhand, then, need not have anything to do with your ability to beat your friend on the courts next Saturday. What it does have to do with is your appraisal of yourself.

Initially, that is. Because once the autocomp has lifted your competence to a certain level, the temptation to "go public" often becomes too strong to resist. It's a rare individual who can perfect a skill in private and not eventually feel obliged to show it off to others.

Autocompers are not always aware that they are competing, and many people who use autocomps regularly would be surprised to hear that they are competing at all. A pianist who practices a piece of music over and over again until he achieves what he considers both technical perfection and a valid interpretation of the composer's intent may not realize that he's involved in an autocomp. In essence, however, each time he practices the piece, he sets a new goal for himself, and each time he is successful in improving his rendition of the piece he also enhances his sense of self-esteem, increases his confidence in himself as a pianist, and motivates himself to strive for even greater achievement.

Wanda Collins, whom we met at the cocktail party, is an excellent example of an autocomper. She is not a particularly good athlete and plays tennis more as a business expedient rather than for its intrinsic interest to her. Thus, she continues to play even though she rarely wins. In order to have a sport in which she could develop competence and thus increase her sense of self-esteem, she took up jogging, building up her stamina and endurance and finally her speed. She did this at her own pace, without anyone's paying attention to her, and she felt increasingly good about herself while she practiced. Now she is ready to go public. All her friends know that she has been jogging all along, but now she's going to enter a marathon. She obviously won't finish first, but that doesn't matter to Wanda: as an autocomp, in this case finishing the race will be a victory in itself. The basic benefit of this is the sense of well-being she will derive from having participated and reached her own internally determined goal.

We should realize that autocomps can encompass many kinds of activity and occur throughout our lives, not just on the playing field. The person who prides himself on completing a challenging crossword puzzle or collecting paperweights also derives this same type of gratification and enhancement of self-esteem.

Goal Vaulting

The person who engages in autocomps in a productive manner has learned how to set himself or herself a reasonable goal and how to go about capturing it. Unfortunately, many people who practice autocomps regularly do so in a nonproductive and ultimately self-defeating manner.

It's ironic that, in an autocomp, where you might think losing is impossible because you yourself comprise the entire field of runners, so many people manage to come in constantly last. For many autocompers, competing with themselves is an opportunity neither for practice nor avoidance, but merely for reiterating an already established feeling of worthlessness. People who are continually unsuccessful in their autocomps are what I call "Goal-Vaulters."

The Goal-Vaulter is the person who is not content with achieving a reasonable goal, but must go on to achieve ever greater, ever more outlandish ones, because he or she is unable to be satisfied with any achievement. In this sense, the Goal-Vaulter is fixated on the process of competition without paying true attention to the goal. (Many professionals and executives suffer from this syndrome.) This is obviously an unhealthy form of competition because before being able to enjoy the psychological benefit of achieving one goal, the Goal-Vaulter is compelled to move on to the next.

"Climb every mountain" may be a laudable maxim, but when it is interpreted to mean that the last mountain you have just climbed was not worth the trip, then the climber is in a dangerous double-bind. On the one hand, he is obliged to climb the next mountain because it promises to give satisfaction, but on the other hand he knows very well from past experience that, no matter how many goals he vaults, they will all prove disappointing in the end.

Jill, a young, energetic physician, was the envy of her colleagues and friends. At the age of twenty-nine, she had a doting husband, a healthy new baby, and a secure private practice in her specialty—radiology. To the casual observer, she was the Golden Girl, riding the crest of personal and professional success.

Inside, however, she was miserable.

When she came to me for help, Jill was an exceedingly troubled young woman. Fidgety and downcast, she confessed that the successes she had accumulated meant nothing to her; she was, in fact, considering both quitting her job and filing for divorce.

"I don't know what it is, Dr. Ruben," she complained. "Gary is a wonderful husband and father. We've been married for three years, with no problems. He's a hard worker and has been really helpful to me—especially since the baby came last year. But I don't love him anymore. I just can't stand what I'm doing, at home or at work."

She laughed nervously. "You know," she continued, "it's almost as if I don't want to be happy. Every time I get what I want, I don't want it anymore."

I asked Jill to expand upon this revealing comment. It turned out that dissatisfaction with success had been a pattern in her life since she was a child. A direct, aggressive competitor, she found herself consistently dismissing compliments and poking fun at the laurels she had gained. Every step she had taken she saw as merely a prelude to the next step, in a perpetual cycle of overreaching. In high school she had been a straight-A student, but she did not enjoy high school and she couldn't wait to get on to college. In college she made Phi Beta Kappa, but saw it only as a way to get into medical school. In medical school she yearned to be an intern, and during her internship she felt herself only biding time until her residency. When that too became boring, she decided it was because what she really wanted was to get married. Gary and she were married, therefore, while she was still a resident.

But neither marriage nor motherhood, which came two years later, solved her problem. Three years after the wedding, Jill had become impatient again. Her spouse had ceased to interest her, and she had come to the conclusion that what she needed now was a new husband. At this point she ended up in my office—frustrated, bored, and unhappy.

Jill's type of discontent is not uncommon among Dag competitors—especially if they have come from a family background of similarly strong competitive urges—and it is particularly prevalent among professionals and executives.

I asked her to talk about her childhood, and what she revealed confirmed my suspicion that her obsession with achievements had started well before her whiz-kid high-school days.

An only child, Jill was born late in their marriage to successful, hard-driving parents who always seemed to have more time for their careers than for her. Ever since she could remember, Jill admitted, they had shown only a passing interest in her achievements. Her father, a banker, was detached and aloof, while her mother, a publishing executive, acted like a meddling and hypercritical judge.

While neither parent had given Jill the approval she needed, it was her mother's negative responses that really hurt her. "I never could please her," she recalled. As early as grammar school, she had worked hard to impress her parents, but had been rewarded with shrugs, silence, or outright criticism. No matter how well she competed, her mother remained unmoved. Neither her Phi Beta Kappa key nor her acceptance by a prestigious medical school had

had any effect on her mother, and, not surprisingly, it wasn't long before Jill herself ceased to consider her successes important.

She was caught in an agonizing dilemma: needing desperately to "come in first," but unable to believe that coming in first meant anything. So frequently had she been denied approval that, when she received it later in life, she could not believe it was deserved.

"I don't deserve to be content," she was really saying to herself. "Therefore, I am not content, and I have to move on to something else."

Probably her unmet need for approval was a principal reason for her initial attraction to Gary. Unlike her parents, he was extremely impressed with her, and as a husband very solicitous. For a while this seemed to be what she wanted, but then the childhood pattern reasserted itself, and she found herself, ironically, longing for the very denial she had so abhorred in her mother.

So accustomed had she become to mistreatment that she did not know what to make of applause. She expressed her confusion about Gary in a telling phrase: "He's just too good to me!"

In therapy I helped Jill to see that, by demanding that Gary be less solicitous, she was actually trying to elicit a response to which, however uncomfortable it made her feel, she had grown accustomed: the response of rejection. In conjoint sessions with Gary, I helped him understand what had been happening to his wife and how his ostensibly generous behavior had only aggravated her problem. He, I discovered, had been unwilling to compete with Jill at all, believing he was no match for his intelligent, successful spouse. Instead of giving her a realistic mixture of approval and disapproval, he had merely given in to her every whim, and this, predictably, had caused her to lose respect for him.

Since both Jill and Gary were committed to saving their marriage, we entered a phase of couples therapy in which Gary learned to make reasonable demands and offer the limited approval Jill needed rather than the adulation he thought she wanted. Jill responded well. As Gary became more of a friend and less of a cheering squad, he regained her respect and they reestablished the love and affection that had brought them together.

So while the Goal-Vaulter's obsession with achievement may stem from a childhood deficient in approval, such a competitive malaise cannot be cured by going overboard the other way. What the Goal-Vaulter needs is what any healthy competitor needs: real-

istic, balanced appraisal of how he or she is behaving. Jill ultimately learned to attend to both the process and the goals of competition rather than being overinvolved with either. With this new
attitude she was able to appreciate Gary's realistic input, and she
came to value the successes of her daily life without having to continually search about for new goals.

All of us move from one success or failure to another
throughout our lives. To the extent that our successes have little
meaning for us in terms of our psychic economy and our sense of
self-worth, then we are compelled to leap on to new endeavors
without pausing to savor the psychologically sweet taste of success.

This is the Goal-Vaulter's tragedy.

Using Autocomps Successfully

Clearly, anyone can compete with himself or herself as well as
with others. What is most interesting about autocomps is the ways
in which individual competitors use them either to enhance their
own competitive edge or to opt out of competition (external competition, that is) altogether.

Generally speaking, the more aggressive the competitor, the
more likely he or she is to use autocomps as practice and preliminary training for interpersonal combat. Conversely, the less aggressive the competitor, the more likely he or she is to use them as
a way of escaping interpersonal combat.

Since we generally think of competition as a healthy phenomenon—or at least a necessary evil—we might conclude that the
persons who use autocomps most effectively are those for whom
testing themselves acts as a kind of preliminary event before the
real test "out there" against the world. Using autocomps as a way
of escaping other competition, we might think, is a sign at best of
timidity, at worst of an unnatural, nonproductive fear.

In fact, however, even the most aggressive, most successful
competitors can be guilty of using autocomps in a nonproductive,
self-defeating manner. And in some cases avoiding competition
may not be at all the unhealthy reaction it seems to be.

*The real test is whether or not you feel comfortable about
yourself as you compete*—be that competition with others or with
yourself. The least aggressive competitor in the world can be successful in a carefully chosen autocomp, while the most aggressive

and successful competitors, if they suffer from the Goal-Vaulter's obsession with overreaching themselves, can be failures. The truly successful autocomper is the person who understands the difference between an achievable and a merely impressive goal, and sets his or her sights accordingly.

The principal attraction of autocomps is that they offer the less aggressive competitor an arena where he or she can win based entirely on his or her own established rules. If you forget the freedom inherent in this situation, however, you will only end up defeating yourself.

It's important to remember that as a type of competition the autocomp can be utilized in many different areas of life. It is to these areas—which I call competitive "arenas"—that we must now turn our attention. We begin with the arena in which we are all first exposed to competition, the one which serves as the youthful competitor's training ground: the home.

PART II
Arenas of Competition

5

THE TRAINING GROUND:
Competition in the Family

A number of years ago, my wife and I were invited to dinner at the home of a couple who had an eight-year-old girl and a boy about two years younger. It was a delightful evening. We had just begun talking about starting our own family, and that gathering might have been designed to illustrate how enriching and pleasant parenthood can be. Not only were our friends' children quiet, obedient, and well-mannered, but when the meal was over, they politely excused themselves, cleared the table, and began doing the dishes!

"How did you ever get them to do that?" I asked our host.

"Oh, it was no effort," he replied. "They started it on their own a few months ago, and they've been doing it a couple of times a week ever since."

"Not just for company?" I asked, a bit incredulous.

"Not at all."

"And you don't reward them for it?"

"We don't pay them, no. They seem to get a great satisfaction out of it, and we figure that's payment enough."

I watched the two youngsters hard at work as we had our coffee and dessert. They seemed like model children. Playing the cynic, I tried to detect whether either of them were being forced to behave in this way, but I had to admit that, as far as I could see, they were both enjoying themselves immensely, just as their parents said.

It wasn't until a few years later that I discovered my cynicism had not been unfounded after all. The mother of the two children called me one day to ask what she described as a "delicate" question. Could her daughter, who was now twelve, make an appointment to see me for psychiatric treatment?

"Why, what's troubling her?" I asked.

She sighed in frustration. "I really don't have a clue. She's got some idea that Bob and I don't love her anymore. She's constantly grumpy with us; she won't even talk to her brother; and I'm sure she's been taking money from my purse."

It would have been unwise for me to treat the daughter of friends, so I referred her to a colleague of mine. After our conversation had ended, I began to wonder what could have gone so wrong since our dinner party. The more I reconstructed the scene that night, the more I realized I had been duped. The generous, cooperative spirit we had witnessed between brother and sister had, I now saw, been a farce adopted for us, for their parents, and perhaps even for themselves. Beneath their calm exteriors, fiercely competitive feelings were being masked.

After the girl had been in therapy for several months, I ran into the mother, who told me she and her husband had been involved in several family sessions with their daughter. The therapist had helped the parents to understand that the girl's resentment of her family, and her brother in particular, had started not since our last visit, but years before.

"It's amazing," she said. "She's felt jealous of him since he was born. The doctor said that they had been competing for our affection for years."

Armed with this information, I began to see the dishwashing episode in a different light. I now saw their race into the kitchen to help clean up as symbolic of their hidden race for their parents' approval.

And I could reconstruct the way the situation might have come about:

1. Born two years before her brother, the daughter is the apple of her parents' eye—until he intrudes.

2. She reacts initially with anger, with overt jealousy, but this only makes her parents angry. Afraid she will lose their love, she takes another tack, striving to become the Perfect Child, the child they would have to love more than her rival.

3. When the brother becomes old enough to realize that his sister's good behavior leads to parental approval, he joins her and begins to compete for the crown of Most Loved Child.

4. After a year or so of this, they're both washing dishes in a frenzy. Their parents are delighted with the situation, and fail to realize that their approval of this "good" behavior merely reinforces the rivalry between their children.

5. Finally, the siblings are locked into a constant rivalry masquerading as mutual aid. On the surface there is friendly cooperation; inside is a core of fierce—and fiercely disguised—competitiveness.

6. This apparent harmony was disrupted as the daughter reached puberty. She became dissatisfied with her physical appearance and was plagued by feelings of inferiority; at the same time, her mother seemed to be having higher expectations and to be placing greater demands on her. As a result, she felt she had become a loser and that her parents loved her brother more. Soon after, she developed the symptoms that caused her mother to seek help.

The more I thought about it, the more I realized that, with some modifications, this pattern of sibling rivalry was all too prevalent in the modern family.

My Brother the Other: Trouble in the Nest

So pervasive is sibling rivalry in human families that the "battle of brothers" has for centuries been a recurrent motif in popular culture and folklore. From Cain and Abel in Biblical times, to the story of Romulus and Remus quarreling over the foundation of ancient Rome, through the nineteenth-century French novel by Dumas of the ill-fated Corsican twins, to the saga of the rival gunfighter brothers in the comic Western film *Cat Ballou* and to more recent TV portrayals ("The Brady Bunch," "Eight Is Enough," "Different Strokes"), the notion of fraternal strife has played easily as significant a role in the popular imagination as the more frequently acknowledged notion of brotherly love. We pay elaborate lip service to the latter, but the former is closer to the reality of many family situations. We seldom realize, moreover, how far-reaching the effects of sibling rivalry can be. I have seen numerous patients suffering from its long-term effects who think they are being plagued by something else entirely.

Richard, for example, was a young man who came to me complaining of problems in his dating relationships. He was a junior in college at the time, and he hadn't had a satisfying relationship with a woman since high school.

"Whenever I get into a close relationship," he told me, "I end up driving the girl away. I don't know why, but I always seem to do something or say something that ruins it."

Richard's family structure, as it turned out, was at the root of his romantic failures. He was the third of four brothers in a very competitive, upwardly mobile family, and since he was very young he had always been low man on the sibling totem pole. No matter how hard he had tried, his brothers seemed always to edge him out: they got better grades, were more athletic, had more friends. This pattern persisted throughout their youthful lives together. In short, Richard was an Indinag competitor in a family of Dags.

It was not surprising that, out of this background of being considered the family failure, Richard developed an inability to succeed outside the family as well. Because he had grown up thinking he was unable ever to win out over his siblings, he looked for failure as an adult as well. When he got close to a woman, he unconsciously set up ways to destroy the relationship. He couldn't handle success, because it was something for which his background simply hadn't prepared him. In a sense, he couldn't believe that any woman might like him, so he kept telling her in subtle ways why she shouldn't. In an initial series of individual psychotherapy sessions, Richard came to see how he demeaned himself. He eventually pushed each girlfriend toward another relationship. I was also able to point out how he utilized the role of habitual loser as a way to gain pity, support, and nurturance from his family. Although this worked within the family setting, it didn't succeed in his romantic relationships.

I decided that Richard would benefit from group therapy. In the course of intensive psychological interaction with several other patients, he came to identify his dysfunctional Indinagish patterns and to develop a more realistic appraisal of himself. After a year as a group member, he began to date a young woman whom he eventually married.

With this ultimate success, he learned to deal with his family more appropriately. He no longer needed to be indirect and non-aggressive as a defense. As he became more secure in his relationship with his new wife, he became less awestruck by his brothers' supposed accomplishments and more concerned with his own internal goals. He thus evolved through treatment into a Dinag competitor, and for the first time in his life allowed himself to experience success.

Or take the case of Danny Marchant in Chapter 1. Danny's excessive drinking may seem like a peculiarly adult problem. Actually, although he only began to drink heavily in his twenties, the cause of his alcohol dependency reaches back into the earliest days of his childhood. His rivalry with his sister Barbara, an adept Indag competitor, was so traumatic for him as a youngster that he carried signs of his suffering into maturity. He turned to drinking as a way of opting out of further competition not only with her, but with her husband Perry as well. While he would sneer at the idea that he was rivalrous with Barbara and Perry, his disdain of their situation and social status was actually his way of competing with them.

This demonstrates one of the most curious aspects of sibling competition: the fact that, for the sibling who sees himself or herself as a loser, very little in the way of future successes can offset that notion. The effects of early failure—or perceived failure—are extremely tenacious.

Danny, for example, could hardly be considered a failure in any objective sense. He is bright, fairly successful, and considered by many to be an excellent lawyer. But in his own mind he is still little Danny, the kid brother who can't compete with his sister— and it is that image which is driving him toward self-destruction. He has, over the years, taken Barbara's Indagish tools for himself as a way to attempt to best Barbara. Since he is unable to, he is continually reinforced as a loser in that relationship; alcohol is his way of dealing with this sense of failure.

In homes in which all the children feel frankly and equally loved, sibling rivalry, although it still exists, seldom becomes a major problem, because the children can be confident that parental affection is not predicated on this or that form of acceptable behavior. They can then use sibling rivalry as a way of learning how to test themselves in competitive situations. If they are sure of their parents' love, siblings can use each other as practicing partners or "loving enemies," and so spur each other on to a better realization of their individual talents without the fear that failure in some particular endeavor will mean the loss of parental affection.

Such homes, however, seem to be the exception rather than the rule, since by and large parents tend to play favorites with their children. This has the effect of making many children, whether they generally win or generally lose, exiles in their own land. Parents frequently use the children against one another to point out defects or shortcomings. Such comparison is almost always detrimental: saying "Why can't you be more like your sister?" may satisfy a need for control on the parent's part, but it will do nothing to ensure that the "inferior" child shapes up. On the contrary, the child will only resent the "good" sibling all the more.

Invidious comparisons of this sort, however, are only one of many ways in which parents attempt to manage and control the behavior of their children. In the next section we'll look at a few more ways.

The Sins of the Parents

You remember the parents I mentioned at the beginning of this chapter, and how they reacted to seeing their children helping out in the kitchen. They loved it, and felt no compunction about expressing their approval for what was, unknown to them, an intensely competitive situation.

This kind of parental reaction to sibling rivalry is very common. Either because they don't see what is going on or because they want to set their children against one another (the "divide and conquer" theory of parenting), parents often allow unhealthy competitive games to go on right under their noses. Naturally, the children then pick up the message that "Mommy and Daddy like us to compete" and intensify their efforts.

Why would parents ever encourage rivalry between their children?

Some parents, of course, sincerely believe that in a dog-eat-dog world, learning to compete is essential; they encourage rivalry as a way of ensuring that their children acquire the quasi-military skills they believe are necessary to social survival. Others, like the mother and father of our dishwashing "team," don't perceive what is happening and inadvertently encourage rivalry in the mistaken belief that what they are really encouraging is cooperation.

But almost all parents, when they encourage rivalry, do so at least partly because it benefits *them* psychologically, whatever it may do to the children. Parents are every bit as much in need of approval, affection, and support as their children, and in many cases, unfortunately, they are able to get this most easily by nourishing divisiveness within the home. If none of the children can be really certain of their parents' undivided affection, they will all strive harder to please—which means that the parents will be showered with the very attention they require.

The Alliance System: "Divide and Conquer"

The types known as "Daddy's Girl" and "Mama's Boy" are illustrative of how divisiveness often works. A Daddy's Girl is a young woman who so idealizes and is so attached to her father that she is unable to form a relationship with any other man. A Mama's Boy, on the other hand, is a young man whose need for affection and approval can be satisfied only by the woman who satisfied it when he was a child: his mother. Both types are examples of a one-to-one alliance set up within the family structure as a way of managing affection. Such alliances, which are quite common, illustrate not only the need on the part of all family members—parents and siblings alike—for approval, but the ease with which that need can be distorted to serve the purposes of interpersonal competition.

Let us say I'm one of two siblings. If, on an unconscious level, we are uncertain of our parents' love, and they in turn, because of their own insecurity, are uncertain of ours, one way we can convince ourselves that everybody is "equally" loved is to set up a system of dual alliances in which one parent takes me as the favorite and the other parent takes my brother or sister. We will all then have one "best friend" who can be relied upon for approval and support. Everybody will win.

Or will they? The alliance system gives everybody an equal shot at affection, yes, but it does so usually at a terrible cost to the participants. Not only does a mother-son or father-daughter alliance tend to isolate family members into opposing camps, but it also sets up an internal confusion on everyone's part. Being Daddy's Girl may make me feel great about Daddy and about myself, but the inevitable outcome of such a situation is that I will see myself as *not* Mommy's Girl—that is, as a stranger and maybe even an enemy to my other, unallied parent. I don't have to point out how damaging psychologically that can be for parent and child alike: Cain's murder of Abel, for example, was the result of what he thought was an alliance between his brother and God. Like a father playing favorites, God accepted Abel's offering to Him while rejecting Cain's, thus provoking a fatal rivalry between the two brothers.

So the alliance system seems to create just as much resentment and suspicion as it does confidence. Moreover, in many cases alliances are made only to be broken when personalities or situations change. I may be Daddy's Girl this month and Mommy's Little Helper next month, while my brother, who is Mama's Boy today, may form a pact tomorrow to be Daddy's Little Man. Obviously, these shifting loyalties produce confusion and instability within the family.

To make things even worse, alliances are seldom formed on the basis of felt similarities. Almost without exception, a parent wants a specific child to be his or her ally not simply on the basis of the child's own merits (though that surely will have something to do with it), but because at a certain time and in a given situation he or she needs that child as an ally against the spouse. Parents who are having competitive or other problems with each other very often transfer these problems to their children, and enlist one or another child as the current favorite to gain support for their own positions. This creation of a parent/child coalition against the other parent is called *triangulation* by family therapists.

Such a situation can be very distressing indeed. I once had a patient who endured extreme stress throughout his childhood not because of sibling rivalry (he was an only child), but because of the wider, more "adult" rivalry of his parents. They seemed constantly on the verge of breaking up and used the boy mercilessly as, alternately, a pawn and a referee in their own competitions.

Larry knew very little of a parent's unmitigated affection; what he knew all too well was that every time his parents fought he would be drafted as an ally by one parent and rejected as a bad example by the other. If he broke a plate or spilled a glass of milk during one of their competitive periods, his father would smile indulgently and his mother would denounce him as "a slob like your father." If he asked for movie money during one of those periods, his father would rant about his being a "spendthrift like your mother." Larry grew up, therefore, in a bewildering fog of name-calling and denunciations. His parents' inability to resolve their own rivalry made him conclude, like many children in similar positions, that neither parent really loved him, that he was somehow responsible for it, and that he himself was a combination of all the most negative qualities of each of his parents.

The Oedipal Knot

Occasionally the alliance system leads to severe pathological problems, because in their manipulation of their children, parents unwittingly tighten the bonds of affection so firmly that they cannot thereafter loosen them without causing emotional havoc all around. Sometimes this happens when the children are half grown, but more frequently it occurs—or begins—early in the child's life. Parent-child affection in the early years, as Freud pointed out long ago, is fraught with hidden motives and inadmissible yearnings. Freud's identification of the Oedipal triangle as a keystone in human psychological development has been debated fervently for years, and I don't want to add to that discussion here. I do want to show, however, how the Oedipal problem may be interpreted not only in the light of our secret sexual drives, but also of our strongest competitive urges.

Freud felt that, unconsciously, all boys want to marry their mothers and, therefore, supplant and eliminate their fathers—the chief competitors for the mother. He called this desire the "Oedipus complex" after the mythical Greek king who had done just that. He used the phrase "Electra complex" (named after the Greek maiden who instigated the murder of her mother to avenge her father) to describe what he felt was a complementary desire in girls.

Now, there is plenty of evidence that such unconscious desires do exist. Four- and five-year-old children are fascinated by the notion of marrying the parent of the opposite sex and doing away with the same-sex parent. They will frequently remark that "If you die I'll marry Mommy (or Daddy)," and it's clear that a good deal of their fantasy play has to do with fulfilling the Oedipal design.

What is interesting in the context of this book's theme is that the Oedipus or Electra complex may be seen as a kind of grandly exaggerated act of rivalry: the ultimate distortion of the alliance system, one which aims at ensuring not only a complete but also a permanent bond of loyalty. For boys, wanting to marry or sleep with Mommy is clearly a desire to beat Daddy at his own game, while for girls union with Daddy is prized not simply for its own sake but for the competitive edge it will give them over Mommy.

In the case of young children, it is usually sufficient for a parent to deal with these desires through casual good humor or indulgent explanations. Yet we must never forget the intensity or seriousness of these competitive urges in children. Sometimes, unfortunately, this humorous or superficial management is totally inadequate, especially in cases where the unconscious desire to do away with one parent seems to bear fruit—as in cases of death, separation, or divorce. To a child in the Oedipal stage of development, his or her fantasies about doing away with a parent will seem fulfilled if that parent suddenly dies or leaves, giving the child the impression that he or she is actually responsible for the parent's loss.

Robbie, for example, was a six-year-old boy whom I treated during my training at the Child Psychiatry Clinic of Walter Reed General Hospital in Washington, D.C. When his mother brought him to me, he had started wetting his bed, was suffering from night terrors (an extreme form of nightmares), and was refusing to go to school.

Robbie's father, I learned, had recently been killed in action in Vietnam, and what our therapy sessions disclosed was that Robbie felt a direct responsibility for his death. While his father was at the front, the boy had grown accustomed to falling asleep each night in his mother's bed, and just before the news of his father's death reached home, he had begun to wonder aloud, "If Daddy didn't come home, could I marry you, Mommy?"

The tragedy hit him with special severity, for it seemed to Robbie that perhaps his "bad thoughts" had actually caused his father's death. "I won," he was thinking to himself. "I beat Daddy for good, and that's terrible." It was a victory without delight, because it was one thing to beat his father in the fantasized Oedipal struggle and quite another to be rid of him entirely. Since children of Robbie's age have not yet fully learned that thinking or wishing a thing does not automatically make it so, they may become very damaged psychologically when an unallowable fantasy seems to turn into fact.

When Robbie's competitive rivalry with his father seemed to lead to tragedy, he became confused about his relationship with his mother as well. Like most children of his age, Robbie had at times wished his mother harm, seeking to punish her as she had sometimes punished him. This was an entirely natural parent-child competition for power and control. But after his father's death, Robbie became fearful that his "bad thoughts" and resentment of his mother might lead to her death as well. It was at this point that he decided he could not let her out of his sight, and began to refuse to go to school.

Fortunately, treatment helped Robbie; had he not received professional help, it is conceivable he would have become a chronically anxious, neurotic adult. He might have become frozen in his competitive efforts throughout life for fear of the devastation he might wreak on others if he permitted his full competitive anger to be released. So it becomes clear that, for the child, losing the Oedipal competition is much more healthy in the end than winning it.

Other children—and some parents—have different problems in unraveling the Oedipal knot. In cases where severe rivalry between parents focuses around a child, the child can sometimes be used as a sexual pawn by one or the other parent. In these cases the trauma can be quite severe.

The many cases of incest between fathers and daughters and mothers and sons which are currently coming to light attest to the facility with which, in certain situations, the parent-child alliance system can have disastrous results. Incest, indeed, is a kind of final distortion of family competition. Generally because of problems with his or her spouse, the parent achieves a particularly harmful sexual alliance with a child for the purposes of spiting the partner or gaining the gratification lacking in the marital relationship.

The child in these cases is forced to compete in a direct and aggressive manner with the same-sex parent. Yet for a girl to win Daddy's sexual love destroys not only any possible bond to Mommy, but the bond to Daddy as well. Since our culture places heavy moral sanctions against this form of sexual competition, all of the participants in an incestuous game come out losers.

John, for example, was a middle-aged father who came to me seeking help because he was worried about his incestuous feelings toward his fifteen-year-old daughter, Cathy. Investigation of his case revealed that his problem was directly related to his perception of himself as a "loser" vis-à-vis his highly competitive wife, Betty.

John and Betty had married during college, at a time when neither of them appeared overtly competitive; they were both Indinag competitors who were attracted to each other by what they saw as a mutual gentleness and sensitivity. A combination of luck, resourcefulness, and appropriate use of his Indinagish tools, however, had made John quite successful over the years, and Betty, in order to keep up with him, had begun to spend more and more time away from home, engaged in philanthropic activities that gave her a sense of her own importance and "success." Eventually, she became the head of a national philanthropic organization, and John and his daughter were left alone together even more frequently.

In retrospect, it was easy to see that at this point Betty had lost interest in the marriage, forcing both John and Cathy to look to each other for the support and affection they were not getting from her. John began to see a kind of teenaged Betty in his daughter, while Cathy became far more of a "Daddy's Girl" than she had ever been. Soon Cathy had become the wife that John had lost, and it wasn't long before John began to entertain the incestuous fantasies that brought him to me.

Now, such fantasies are not uncommon in family situations such as this, and since John came to me before anything overt had actually happened between him and his daughter, I was able to reassure him that he was not "going crazy," as he feared. But the marriage could not be saved. Family counseling sessions made it clear that Betty was uninterested in continuing the relationship with her husband, and that she had chosen competitiveness in the outside world as a way of bringing matters to a head. Cathy, for her part, was able to see that her increased attention to her father had been a way of retaliating against a mother whom she perceived as having abandoned her. The whole family came to see the near tragic alliance between father and daughter as the next-to-last link in a chain of highly competitive events. The final link, as it turned out, was divorce.

The alliance system, in its benign or pathological forms, is one of the most common ways in which parents control their children and vice versa. It is not the only way of manipulating behavior, however, and in the next section I want to discuss another method of control, one which some parents employ ostensibly to defuse competitive behavior. I call it *slotting*.

Slotting

The actor Roddy MacDowell recently made a TV guest appearance on "The Carol Burnett Show" playing Carol's long-lost brother, a Pulitzer Prize-winning author. Most of the skit's humor derived from the fact that the parents were far more interested in the antics of a puppy they had just acquired than in their son's unexpected return. Throughout the skit he tried to tell them about his writing, but they paid him only casual attention. Finally, the bewildered author left.

"Go ahead, son," said the father absentmindedly. "Go win another prize."

This comedy situation effectively illustrates the mechanism of slotting, a manipulative technique to keep each child in a multichild family in a restricted—and therefore manageable—place.

Aside from parental affection, many siblings are apt to compete over toys, grades, television programs, friends, and a host of other "prizes." In some families, unchecked competition threatens to lead to chaos, and as a result parents sometimes manipulate their children's rivalries so that each child is continually judged "best" in a particular area or "slot" and inferior to his or her siblings in other slots.

The Roddy MacDowell character in the skit had been slotted by his parents into the Wandering Scholar role, while his sister had been cast into the Dutiful Daughter position. The unconscious parental intent was that the daughter should not be interested in travel or books and that the son should not be interested in anything so "domestic" as their new puppy. When the father advised his son to go win another prize, he was really telling him to keep out of the domestic slot and stay where he performed "best."

I have seen numerous instances in which parents of multichild families arbitrarily assign roles to their children in this manner. Bobby becomes the brainy one, Kay is the athlete, Georgie is musical, Fran likes to work with her hands, and so on. Although these descriptions may originally have been based on observations about each child's particular talents or penchants, very often the slots turn into straitjackets that reduce growth. Bobby realizes he is not supposed to be good at football, and so must not enter that field of endeavor if he is to retain the approval of his parents; similarly, Fran gets the covert message she can't possibly play the trumpet as well as Georgie and must not even try to develop in this direction.

Slotting is a convenience for parents, a way of defusing sibling competition by giving each child an arena in which he or she can always be seen as a winner. There's no doubt that the technique initially reduces friction in the home, but in the long run it may even aggravate sibling rivalry. No parent is really capable of determining his or her children's interests so precisely that a particular "slot" will always feel comfortable to them. Children, like all other humans, are flexible creatures; when forced to restrain themselves through artificial controls, a potentially disruptive family situation is created.

Para-Parents

So far I have been describing competition in what is commonly referred to as the nuclear family, consisting of a mother, a father, and one or more children who live with them. Fewer and fewer families today, however, fit that particular pattern as the number of "broken" and "extended" families of various types increase. At this point I want to mention a few of the competitive problems associated with these different family structures.

In the traditional nuclear family, control and responsibility are shared by two biological or adoptive parents who are their children's principal source of emotional nourishment and the main focus of their competitiveness vis-à-vis authority. As we have seen, even such relatively simple arrangement gives rise to many confusions and shifting alliances. Today, as the nuclear family increasingly shares its parenting role with other forms of childrearing, the confusions inherent in family life can be aggravated by the presence of people whom I call "para-parents" (substitute or surrogate parents).

Sometimes the parents themselves function as para-parents. When couples divorce, for instance, one parent generally retains custody of the children while the other parent ceases to exert a constant daily influence on them. In effect, he or she becomes a para-parent. And since divorce frequently signifies the end of a willingness to put mutual welfare before personal desires, the former spouses often compete viciously with each other—almost always at the expense of the children.

This is not to suggest that divorce is a thoroughly damaging choice in every unhappy marital situation. In many cases, it is the healthiest and most productive option open to warring partners; if the marriage has been one long battle, separation is obviously preferable to continued daily enmity. It's a mistake to imagine that staying together "for the children" is a wise choice, since both parents and children are bound to suffer if the only thing keeping the union going is the parents' bond to their offspring.

However, the fact that divorce is often the best choice does not mean that it is ever an easy or an untroubled one. The incidence of "good" divorces—separations characterized by mutual amity and regard—is pretty low in my experience. No matter how necessary the split may have been, divorced people all too often use their children to "get back" at their former partners; in a pathological extension of the alliance system, they may try to establish complete control over their children not out of affection for them but to spite the ex-spouse.

This perversion of parental love—a direct result of competition—can be disastrous. Not uncommonly, one parent will attempt to intimidate the other with a threat that he or she will never see a child again unless certain demands are met; there have also been recent cases in which one parent, desperate to win out over his former spouse, kidnapped his own child. And finally, the length and bitterness of some custody battles testify amply to the anguish which competition between ex-spouses can elicit.

Other sources of conflict engendered by competition complicate the picture even in relatively stable marriages. Chief among them are in-laws, who as grandparents constitute a type of para-parent. Far from being free of rivalries, in-laws and grandparents are often extremely competitive.

The marriage of a child, which is so often portrayed as an occasion for joy, in reality can be a traumatic and threatening event for some parents. Unconsciously this means not that they have succeeded in raising a desirable human being, but that they have failed to hold on to that child's love. Marriage thus becomes a betrayal, and the new spouse is perceived as a potentially serious competitor for their child's love. When the spouse picks up on this antagonism, he or she often responds defensively by preferring his or her own "side" of the family over the hostile in-laws. Often, too, in-laws will compete with the parents of their new son- or daughter-in-law. This can create a potentially chaotic situation: I have seen in-laws so antagonistic to each other that they have actually precipitated the breakup of a marriage. So uncertain are they of their own children's love that as they cause the breakup of the marriage they risk losing it entirely should the child ever fully realize the parents' role in the situation.

Grandchildren are often in the middle of this kind of competition, surrounded by "doting" grandparents whose motivations are rooted less in kindness and concern than in a need to ensure respect and affection for themselves. I remember the case of one set of very wealthy grandparents who were upset by the realization that they figured less highly in their grandchildren's estimation than the grandparents from the other side of the family. Their response was to lavish expensive gifts on the children in a blatant attempt to buy their loyalty. This worked for a while, but the less wealthy grandparents, who were far more secure in their own positive feelings toward the children, still remained the favorites, though the activities of their well-off rivals caused them considerable discomfort. The situation was resolved only when the wealthy couple's son—the children's father—succeeded in convincing his parents that they were placing an unfair burden on their grandchildren by forcing them to choose between them and his wife's parents. What's more, as he pointed out, their tactics weren't having the desired effect anyway. He advised his parents to spend more time with the children instead; they began to do so, and were pleasantly surprised to discover that this earned them far more respect than the expensive gifts had ever done.

As we have seen, competition is so ubiquitous in even the most "loving" of homes that it sets the very tone of daily activity, establishing positive and negative patterns for years to come. The home therefore may be seen as a kind of crucible in which the problems of adulthood and the patterns of adult competition are first formed. No matter how old we grow, the need for approval is constant. In attempting to fulfill that need, however, most adults prove themselves to be what they were at the start: rivalrous, possessive children competing for love.

We like to think of love as something unbounded, unlimited—and yet we compete for it as if it were a scarce and ever-diminishing natural resource. It almost never occurs to us that it is possible for a parent to love two, three, or even ten children with equal intensity. Because Daddy loves my sister very much does not necessarily mean that he loves me any less. Unless we understand this important lesson, however, we are condemned to constricted choices, to unsatisfying alliances, to an overemphasis on winning. The tragic irony is that because we feel we must fight for love, we often get little of it in return.

IN LOCO PARENTIS:
Competition in the School

Every year, just as the tulips begin to open and frisbees start to fly, a number of young people on college campuses around the country climb to the top of one of the taller buildings, take a last look at their fellow students crisscrossing the quadrangles below, and hurl themselves to their deaths. As final exams approach, it's almost a statistical certainty that a number of students will succeed in taking their own lives, and that more will make the attempt.

Most of these students, predictably, have not been doing well in school for a while; they are the casualties of an educational system in which competition for grades is intense and unrelenting. But not all are poor students, which points to an interesting fact about competition in the schools: it is not so much the fact of failure as the anticipatory anxiety over its possibility which leads to such desperate measures as suicide.

I have treated many depressed young people who were unable to contend with the competitive pressures of college. They usually had in common a self-image that almost ensured failure, no matter how well they were actually doing in school. In general, their lack of self-esteem could be traced to an early failure to compete successfully in the family arena. Unfortunately, they had carried this experience with them into the school setting, where it made them not only academically but socially self-destructive.

The First Crisis

Among the earliest pressures encountered are those produced by the changeover from family to kindergarten or nursery school—a transition period I call the early school crisis, because it involves a recognition which many young children have trouble accepting, namely that, somewhere between the ages of five and seven, the rules of the game have changed.

Family interactions, especially sibling rivalry, can be diffuse and malleable; the fickleness of alternately demanding and doting parents within a shifting alliance system contributes to the child's sense that, sometimes, it is possible to bend the rules in his oi her favor. Learning about competition in the family, then, often means learning more subtle tactics for getting your own way; only rarely do very young children experience situations in which their will is constantly thwarted. Even if the infant must be denied the book of matches it wants, the parent will usually offer a substitute or consolation toy in exchange, and this in a way has the effect of giving the child its way after all.

Thus the entrance into a *group* learning situation can be initially confusing because teachers are seen by young children as para-parents, and yet no teacher can afford to give each child the individual attention and approval it is used to getting at home. Nor can a teacher be subtly manipulated as parents often are into giving a child his or her own way. This becomes a primary lesson of socialization, and of course it is not an entirely happy one.

Carrying the tensions of sibling rivalry into a group setting, the child suddenly discovers that the field of competitors for the para-parent's (teacher's) attention has grown very large, and is apt to interpret the resultant diminution of attention as a denial of love. Some children experience their first competitive stumbling blocks at precisely this stage. The tension they feel at this point is between having their own way by *convincing* the teachers and other students that theirs is the right way, or by subordinating their own needs and *conforming* to the will of the teachers or the group.

Josie presents an example of how damaging the failure to deal with the tensions of the early school crisis can be for a person later in life. An only child, she had come from a home situation in which she was treated like a little princess by both her parents.

Since she was an inventive and imaginative child, she had learned, in the first five years of her life, a whole range of competitive tools to get her way even in those rare situations in which her parents were at first reluctant to go along with her.

When she got to kindergarten, she was at a loss. Since she had never learned to experience frequent rejection, she didn't know what to make of a situation in which other wills were constantly pitted against her own. She became, in desperation, a *convincer,* compensating for what she saw as an obstructive situation by trying to win everyone over, at all times. Whereas at home she had been adept at basically Indinagish competitive techniques, she had to resort, in the less privileged position in which she now found herself, to a range of new Dagish tools—and she was far from comfortable using these direct and aggressive ploys.

Naturally, few of the other children cared to go along constantly with Josie's pronouncements as to how things ought to be done, and she became a social outcast; the Boss, the other children called her. Her dysfunctional behavior continued throughout grade school. By the time she finally came to me for help, about the age of thirteen, she had turned to drugs in an attempt to alleviate the tensions of her unfortunate outsider's position and as a way to gain acceptance from a small subgroup of her peers.

So the transition from a nuclear setting into a group setting can be one of the worst, and earliest, traumas associated with schooling. It is not, of course, the last, for as soon as the young person is actually in the group setting, a new focus of tension begins to predominate: whereas the original tension was between *convincing* and conforming to group pressures, the new tension is between *performing* and conforming. No sooner, then, does the child learn to be part of the group than he comes under pressure to separate himself from the group through achievement.

Performing Versus Conforming

The tension between performance and conformity focuses first on the teacher. On the one hand, the teacher demands that the student perform certain tasks—drawing, counting, writing a theme—to the best of his or her ability. From a very early age, the child is expected to do better than other children in these tasks. Gold stars, pats on the head, high grades, and other signs of approval are given as rewards for excellence in achieving these tasks—that is, for excelling over others.

So, a troublesome tension immediately makes itself felt. At just the point where the child is obliged to learn cooperation and compromise, he is given strong psychic encouragement if he goes his own way, if he succeeds in setting himself apart from the group by virtue of achievement. It's not surprising that many children fail to manage this tension successfully. And the penalties for not achieving can be severe indeed: such a child may be considered a "slow learner" or "underachiever."

Many schools aggravate the child's tension by adopting "tracking" systems whereby the "smart" kids are put into one class and the "dummies" in another. Although theoretically this is supposed to allow every child to compete comfortably with his or her equals, frequently it serves only as a self-fulfilling prophecy whereby the A class learns more quickly because it has been told that it can and the B class falls behind because it has been led to believe it is slow.

The situation is complicated, moreover, by the fact that there is often a contradictory pressure, both from the teacher and from the child's peers, not to perform *too* well, but to conform to a certain modest standard of behavior and academic achievement. "Excellence" in testing is praised by the teacher, but very often it is resented, even denounced, by other children. Thus the child may experience great conflict. If the pressure and anxiety engendered by this conflict become overwhelming, some children actually choose not to compete and opt for mediocrity as a way of avoiding the disapproval of teachers or peers.

So the child, in learning the lessons of socialization, is really learning how to effect a balance between active competition—performance—and the avoidance of a too vigorous competition that would alienate him from others—conformity.

The performance-conformity tension begins early in grammar school, but it's in high school that it makes its most striking appearance. This is predictable, since one of the distinctive characteristics of teenagers is that they are remarkably conformist in their behavior. It's in adolescence that peer pressure is most active, and for good reason: at a time when great physical and emotional flux is making young people constantly uncertain of their very identity, conformity to the norms of a peer group provides comforting reassurance that something, at least, is stable in their world. Wearing the same clothes as their friends or using the same "in" language are ways of saying to the fluctuating personality within, "Hold it now, let's slow things down for a while." Conformity thus becomes a way of managing tension.

But peer pressure is not always so comforting. It can turn into a kind of "fear pressure" quite easily, so that the terror of being thought different, rather than the need for assurance, becomes its principal motivation. This can lead to a host of problems, many of them related to the central issue of social competition.

Early Fear Pressure: Conformity

To ensure their acceptance by the group, some youngsters allow themselves to be drawn into negative and even dangerous situations. So compelling is their need to avoid conditions of invidious excellence that they often prefer to imperil their own safety rather than distort their image of "fitting in" with their peers.

In the movie *Rebel Without a Cause,* for example, James Dean plays a confused adolescent who, because he cannot secure the affection of either of his parents, turns instead to his school group for peer approval. This too fails, as his peers begin to exert fear pressure on him. He enters a series of competitive games with the school tough guy, Buzz. One of these is the famous "chicken race," in which the two boys race cars toward a cliff, with the first one to jump out—to "chicken out" of going over the edge—being declared the loser. Nearing the edge, Buzz jumps first, but because his jacket catches on a handle, he is trapped in the car and killed. Dean is immediately ostracized because he is seen as responsible for his companion's untimely death.

The episode indicates an important point about early fear pressure: the capriciousness, and yet inflexibility, of its rules. In working toward acceptance by the group, Dean is forced to compete in a game which is rigid, arbitrary, and dangerous. He knows this, and if he were not so overcome by the fear of being rejected by the group, he would be able to say, "Look, Buzz, this is a dumb game. We could get killed doing this. Let's try something else instead." The need to conform makes him do something he knows very well is foolish.

This same principle underlies the not infrequent occurrence of injury or death which befalls young people during hazing or initiation rites of some fraternities and sororities or other types of youth groups. As in most adolescent competition, the competitors are working within a "closed" system. There are always strict limits to school-age competition, and what is actively encouraged by the peer-fear pressure I'm describing here is really only a competition to conform within strict limits. If Dean had presumed to call the game itself into question, he would automatically have been declared a loser.

This primary type of fear pressure also explains the importance of cliques in high school society. A clique, like a highly exclusive friendship, provides a person who is unsure of himself with a steady supply of approval even if such approval is unavailable at home. It may therefore be seen as an extension of the alliance system we discussed in the last chapter: a close-knit organization which assures that its members will be winners in spite of external pressures. At least in theory, being a member of an "in crowd" is proof against personal fears of rejection. It's hardly surprising, then, that competition to join such groups—to say nothing of rivalry between groups—can be intense, and that failure to win acceptance by a clique can be extremely demoralizing.

Late Fear Pressure: Performance

I have stated that schooling may be seen as the tension between performance and conformity. An interesting aspect of this situation is that in the realms of higher education the pressure to perform (that is, to compete *beyond* the group norms) frequently begins to take precedence, at least in the academic sphere, over the need to appear the same.

It may seem surprising that, in a chapter ostensibly devoted to a discussion of school, I've said so little thus far about academic performance. This is because, for many students, academic achievement is far less important than social achievement, and remains so almost into high school. In high school, however, the situation changes radically, and students enter a phase I call the late school crisis. Because competition for entrance into college has become so intense, and because a greater proportion of students than ever before plan to go to college, the high school years often are fraught with great tension and interpersonal competitiveness.

Friends begin to realize that, if they are to get into the college of their choice, they will probably have to beat each other out for the few places available.

The case of Janice Collins, Wanda's daughter, is instructive on this point. Janice was a very good student who at the same time felt constantly pressured to excel, both by her highly competitive and successful mother and by the teachers who, knowing she was capable of high achievement, acted on her mother's behalf—in loco parentis—to push her even harder. Janice's problem was not that she couldn't do the work demanded of her; indeed, most of it came quite easily. But she knew that, in order to achieve the high grades she would need to get into a prestigious college, she would have to show herself superior to those of her friends who were in competition with her to get into the same schools. Thus she experienced a classic performance-conformity dilemma: only by outstripping her friends could she really gain their, and her elders', respect.

Much has been written about how "ill prepared" our college students have become in recent years, and this is generally taken to mean that they lack the skills necessary for success in a highly competitive academic environment: they cannot read or write well, are poor in math or science. Naturally, this can be detrimental for a student, but remedial work can often bring skills up to par. A far more serious deficiency is the inability to negotiate the tension management I've just described, and I think it's fair to say that many freshman year "failures" can be attributed not to intellectual laziness or lack of preparation, but to the difficulty of learning that, in this new environment, books rather than peer friendships are paramount.

This is why many "brainy" high school students come into their own in college. They have already begun to prize performance over conformity while in high school (probably because it was the favored quality of their particular clique), and so have less difficulty adjusting than those for whom academic excellence in high school would have ostracized them from their peers. They have been in the lucky position, in other words, of experiencing performance and conformity as equivalents rather than opposites: in their group, poor academic performance was frowned upon, and they were in a best-one-wins situation. This enables them to move from the early to the late type of fear pressure with relative ease.

The experience of these academically successful competitors also suggests that the connection between learning and competition is not always an inverse one. Since you are much more likely to learn your subject well by practicing it frequently, the people who get the most out of their educational experiences may well be those who have been forced, because of competitive pressures, to study with the greatest intensity. The "grind" is not always the smartest or most knowledgeable one in his peer group, but practicing a subject, for whatever motivation, is bound to increase your facility in that subject. For that reason, it's important to note that competitive pressures can often be a spur, a positive incentive, to learning.

Paradoxically, this seems to be more the case in high school, which is frequently considered less competitive than college, than in college itself. Actually, the main competitive pressure in the latter years of high school is directed toward getting those grades which can assure you entrance to college; once you've gotten into college, that pressure disappears. College may, therefore, become a less pressured situation. Except for that percentage of college students who are planning to go on to graduate or professional schooling, the final college transcript is far less important to their future than the senior-year report card is to the future of a collegebound teenager. Thus for some, college is a less competitive situation.

This lessening of the performance-conformity tension sometimes has salutary results. Freed from the requirement to achieve good grades at all costs, many college students find themselves actually enjoying their studies, and an appreciation of learning for its own sake may replace the hunger for grades as a primary motivation of study. For those striving to go to graduate or professional school this is not so. One unfortunate paradox of higher education seems to be that, the longer you spend competing for official designations of approval (grades, diplomas), the longer you must postpone learning for its own sake. Performance thus makes conformists of us all.

Competitive Tools for College Students

Let's look now at the performance-conformity problem with our Competitor's Tool Box in mind. An analysis of the kinds of tools conducive to conformity compared to those conducive to performance will indicate why the late school crisis can be especially grueling to those who were the real social achievers in high school.

High school peer pressure demands that a student employ a great many Indinag tools—such as charm, a sense of humor, and sophistication—in order to be accepted by the crowd. Yet these tools become less useful in the intense academic competition which may exist in college. Except in isolated cases, no amount of eyelash-batting or clever talk is going to ensure a passing grade on a Chemistry exam. In high school, that may not matter so much; in college, it matters a great deal.

What tools, then, *are* useful in college?

I'd say that two types of tools are most valuable to the college-age student competitor (even though I don't recommend both of them): the Dinagish ones and the Indagish ones.

Dag tools, it should be clear, are not likely to be useful in any academic situation. I do know of a few cases where teachers have been intimidated into giving students high marks, but these instances are rare: most of the time, threats and other aggressive tactics are counterproductive.

Much the same thing can be said about Indag tools, though these may be used successfully much more often than Dag tools. Flamboyance and smooth talking in class, for instance, will give a student a "high profile" and may therefore give some teachers a favorable impression. But generally this impression will stand up only if the student is able to prove on paper that his or her apparent interest in the subject was not merely a sham—and for that, you need more than Indag tools.

Some students, of course, compensate for their lack of real preparation or interest by using an Indag tool which has always been a favorite with "poor" students: cheating. Whether it ever proves effective as a long-range technique is questionable. Generally speaking, cheating, like the other Indagish tools, is a makeshift technique which cannot hope to stand competitively against the more direct types of academic effort.

Dinag tools, then, would be my choice as the most appropriate tools to employ in most academic settings. It's hard to beat tenacity, reliance on facts learned, and burning the midnight oil when it comes to a serious academic competition. These, plus as many center-box tools as possible—which, as I've noted, are useful in nearly any competitive situation—help to ensure academic success.

As for the Indinag tools: it's obvious that charm, cajolery, or sophistication would be more useful in a socially competitive setting than in a purely academic one. That's why they're more common in high school and less useful in a more intensive academic setting.

Indinag tools, however, do stand a better chance of being effective in "progressive" educational situations where teacher references and recommendations, rather than strict test scores, are used as the primary index of achievement. Indeed, to compete successfully in a progressive atmosphere, a student often must resort to indirection or be lost in a flurry of Charmers and clever Class Wits.

Only you can really determine what kind of college situation you are in, but generally speaking, if you are competing for letter or number grades, you'll want to favor Dinag tools, whereas if you're competing for a teacher's attention and regard, you'd be wise to consider Indinagish tools. As always, the situational variables will help to dictate which quadrants you should be borrowing from.

But note, in any case, that Dag and Indag tools are of only limited use. In the shadow of the ivory tower, simple aggressiveness is not highly prized.

How, then, can we ensure competitive success for ourselves and our children in the school situation? The answers to that question are many and varied, and it is wise to bear in mind that my identification of the "best" tools to employ provides only an initial, sketchy summary of ways to focus on the issue. As always, it's important to remember that the type of tools required depends on the goals and the situation.

Specific elements of our education system have created a need for a variety of tools and competitive behaviors. Because of the tension between the group-inspired pressure for conformity and the pressure to achieve and excel, a number of students develop competitive problems. Often this is a result of their inability to choose between the competing pressures: they can't negotiate a social system which on the one hand stresses good grades (unfixed or semifixed goals) and which on the other requires only that you achieve a high school diploma (a fixed goal).

The complexity of the classroom situation also contributes to students' difficulties. In the days of the one-room schoolhouse, when every student went along at his or her own rate, Dag tools were probably more important than tools from the other quadrants: the student who was direct and aggressive in putting himself forward most often won the teacher's approval. But it's far more complicated today, and the stresses engendered by modern education may have something at least to do with the students' need to develop flexibility quickly and to learn to borrow tools from quadrants with which they are not familiar.

The educational system, then, is a major force in shaping our children's competitive behavior—often to the dismay of parents who, although they have relinquished some of their authority to the schools, are not always pleased with the values their children learn there. Many parents have a similar difficulty with another major influence on children's attitudes toward competition: the productions, both literary and visual, of the surrounding popular culture. We'll look at how this affects children in the following section.

Tension Management: Helping Your Children

A dominant element in your children's education is the stories they hear at home and in school. The way they learn to deal with each other in the playground, for example, depends not only on the way the teacher tells them to behave; it is intimately connected with the models of behavior they encounter in stories, in books, and on TV. Many children consciously model their behavior on the activities of their favorite fictional heroes, and it's clear that, even for those who are not aware of it, such heroes often play a significant role in their fantasy life.

What kind of role models, then, are we giving our young students-to-be?

The range of children's tales is very wide, but something many of them have in common is the presence of an *obstacle,* either human or natural, to be overcome. From *Jack and the Beanstalk* to *Hansel and Gretel,* many of the stories our children grow up with focus on the attempt of a protagonist—frequently a small protagonist—to struggle against an animate or inanimate foe. Exposure to these stories, according to behavioral scientists, is supposed to teach children such virtues as perseverance, courage, patience, and self-confidence.

You will notice that these are all competitive tools. We can go even further and say that not only is struggle a constant theme, but that winning—as opposed to losing—is also. This seems almost too obvious to mention, yet it points to a crucial element in the way children learn to compete, which is that winning, no matter what the odds and no matter how enjoyable the game, is equated with "being good." The good guys win, the bad guys go to jail or meet with some other miserable fate. Very few stories concern the adventures of happy losers.

Whether the goal is something as mundane as finding a suitable birthday present for a parent or as exotic as dispatching a hungry monster, children's tales generally end in a victory for the young protagonists. Misleading as this may be as a guide to "real" life, this message goes on continually, both in and out of the schools. There are very few parents, in this or any other culture, who tuck their children into bed with stories of the little boy who came in last in the footrace and rejoiced because he'd had such a fine time running it.

This in itself is not bad: in a competitive world, it makes sense to give our children a high opinion of victory. But there is a difference between having a high regard for winning and being merely terrified of losing—of feeling that the "monster" of failure will get you if you do any less than your best—and if we are to give our children truly healthy expectations rather than dangerously impossible dreams, we must keep this distinction in mind.

Unfortunately, what many of our popular books, movies, and television shows suggest is that the best competitive tools in nearly all places, times, and even "dimensions" are the Dagish ones: direct, aggressive, and preferably brutal as well. From King Arthur to Superman, from Robin Hood to Star Wars and Moonraker, the victor is frequently the person who ends up smacking the bad guy louder and harder than the bad guy can smack him. Is it any wonder that children, inundated by such evidence of Might Makes Right, often become ill-adapted to anything but the most Dagish games?

Now, Dagish tools can be extremely useful in certain situations, but as I've noted above, they're not generally terribly useful in school. Success in school usually involves the employment of a range of competitive tools rather than simply a crash course in those of one quadrant; and the most successful academic competitors are those students who borrow readily from all quadrants, including the center.

Parents, in their zeal to ensure that Junior will be a high achiever on this or that examination, often forget this. So eager are they to see their offspring successful that they push them into competitive situations for which they are not prepared, and in which they are bound to fail. Frequently they see this, unconsciously, as a way of correcting their own mistakes—although that translates publicly into the wish that Junior get "all the advantages I never had."

What is crucial for parents to remember is that children are already saddled with numerous competitive problems. Helping the child, therefore, is less a matter of ensuring that he or she has access to all the right Dagish tools than of seeing to it that the youngster is respected and loved for his or her own freely chosen achievements, not merely those considered important by the parents. The consciousness that you are accepted as you are by your parents and your peers is the single most valuable tool any competitor of school age can have.

Beyond this, parents can be aware of the abiding tension in their school-age children between the need to perform and the need to conform. They can be aware that the tension between the two is often frightening and potentially debilitating for young people. And they can remind themselves that, in spite of the necessity to perform, the lure and the comfort of conformity are always very strong, especially in people in the process of testing themselves against an increasingly complicated world. To help their children manage this tension wisely is one of the best gifts parents can give them.

I know that's easier said than done. Especially with teenage children, it's sometimes nearly impossible to show them clearly where their own interests and the interests of their group diverge. Contending with plaintive cries of "Everybody's doing it" has proved the undoing of more than one harried parent, and I have no easy solution for parents who have to deal with a child who seems bent on socially acceptable, perfectly conformist self-destruction.

But sometimes the child's own self-interest can be enlisted in his or her protection. I know a parent who has had some success talking her teenage daughter out of entering potentially dangerous situations simply by reminding her that she was now old enough to make her own decisions rather than allowing a group to make them for her. "I know everybody's doing it," this mother would say, "but that doesn't mean it's right for you!"

I realize that may sound pat, but for my friend and her daughter it wasn't. For them it worked. For them, such a mutual recognition of self-interest as opposed to group interest was an important element in managing the tension between the two types of fear pressure we've been discussing. But it worked for them for a very good reason: beyond all their differences, they genuinely liked each other. They approved of each other, and frequently let each other know it. Because she knew she was loved, the daughter could much more easily than many of her friends deal with the inevitable parent-child differences. Because of this, too, she was able to manage the fear pressure tension, generally, with intelligence and restraint.

Early in childhood, in other words, she had acquired an important center-box tool: a solid, realistic self-confidence which was itself an outgrowth of the knowledge that she was loved and respected by her parents. This knowledge proved, in her dealing with her adolescent friends, of infinitely greater value than theorems, dates, or facts could have been. It gave her the ability to become the kind of student she wanted to be rather than the kind her peer group dictated she ought to be. With that tool alone, she was able to take in her stride the tensions of her school situation, which were terrifying so many of her friends.

Not all children are as fortunate as this young woman was in learning to manage the fear pressure tensions of schooling. I recall a patient of mine named Shirley, whose parents brought her to me when she was sixteen because she was doing poorly in school. The parents were bright, highly motivated professionals who had been extremely successful in their social and business competitions, and wanted the same for their daughter. But Shirley, who had obviously inherited much of their intelligence, was having none of it: for some time she had simply refused to apply herself in school, and as a result, in spite of her high IQ, she was barely passing in most of her subjects.

Her parents' reaction was typical—and typically unsuccessful in motivating her to respond differently. With each new report card showing a lack of academic improvement, they chose to place severe restrictions on her as an "incentive" to do better. In the year before the family finally came for help, Shirley had lost car, TV, phone, and dating privileges, but none of these deprivations had had the desired effect: resentful but uncowed, she had simply failed to respond to her parents' competitive ambitions.

"If she weren't so intelligent," her mother confided, "I wouldn't care so much. But she's so smart, it kills me to see her doing so poorly. That's why we've placed the restrictions on her, but it doesn't seem to help."

"What you're saying," I responded, "is that Shirley is being punished for being bright. If she were less intelligent and making the same grades, she wouldn't be on restriction."

But that was only part of the problem. The real issue was that, as Shirley herself recognized, her parents were trying to re-live their own adolescent years through her. Her mother in particular felt that when she had been Shirley's age, she had never quite lived up to her own academic potential—and she therefore wanted Shirley to make up for it, to become the whiz kid she had failed to become. So she pushed her daughter to excel, and Shirley, in a not uncommon pattern, rebelled against the parental attempt to direct her life. The placing of restrictions on her as punishment was in effect an acknowledgment that all other means had failed. All it did was to add a new difficulty to Shirley's performance-conformity tension: the difficulty of weighing her own needs and desires against those of her parents.

Parents who overidentify with their children's competitive efforts frequently elicit exactly the opposite kind of behavior from that they had hoped to elicit. Shirley's parents, in attempting to encourage a Dagish effort similar to their own, succeeded only in reinforcing their daughter's own Indinagish approach. The best thing they could have done in the situation would have been to retreat, to allow Shirley to manage her school tensions in her own way. Shirley perceived their demands as meddling, and so they actually had a counterproductive effect.

The lesson of this case history is that tension management is often best left up to the individual whose personal concern it is. Demanding that another person—even your own child—live up to your own preordained concepts of "appropriate" competitive behavior can very often cause the person to act in exactly the "wrong" way. Some children, confronted with this kind of situation, refuse to compete at all. Others turn to autocomps. Still others choose to shift arenas, to apply themselves to competition in arenas where they cannot be compared invidiously to their elders.

This last technique is a fairly common way of dealing with the special tensions engendered by overinvolved parents. We have all heard of people who refuse to enter the family business for fear of unfavorable comparison, or who shy away from show business because they are the children of Hollywood stars. This response is especially common in school situations, because such settings offer a great diversity of possible arenas for competition: in terms of competitive intensity, it's a short jump from the blackboard to the football field or the local ice cream parlor, and adolescents shift frequently from one to another of these arenas in their ongoing attempts to balance the contradictory needs of performance and conformity.

Among the most popular of competitive arenas for school-age youngsters is, of course, the athletic one. Athletics often seem as important as academics to the adolescent, and it is the arena of sport—one of the oldest and potentially most aggressive of all competitive arenas—that we will consider next.

7

OUT FOR BLOOD:
Competition on the Playing Field

"Kill the umpire!" "Murder the bums!" "Tear 'em apart!"

Cheers like these—as common as hot dogs in today's big league stadiums—act as reminders of Konrad Lorenz's observation that athletics provide a way for many of us to sublimate the most aggressive, antisocial drives into socially condoned forms. The playing field is one area where the most direct competitive activity is not only sanctioned but, by common consent, applauded. On the playing field, as on the field of war, you are allowed behavior which might even get you jailed off the field.

"Organized battles" is the way one psychologist has recently characterized our modern sports. Indeed, the link between warfare and sports has been noted by many social critics; perhaps it was not inaccurate for one British statesman, in speaking of his nation's athletic prowess, to claim that World War I had been won "on the playing fields of Eton." Today, as in 1914, school sports often serve as a training ground for future, and more violent, competitive efforts.

The process of sublimating aggressive drives into athletics has long been a part of man's history. It took place in Sparta, where the entire population geared itself to readiness for combat by a strict daily regimen of asceticism and exercise. It took place in ancient Rome under the Caesars, with gladiators providing amusement for the mob by killing each other before their eyes. And it was common in more modern times throughout Western Europe:

both Friedrich Jahn's gymnastics system in Napoleonic Germany and Lord Baden-Powell's Boy Scout movement in England may be seen as paramilitary structures, designed to prepare their respective nations for war through strenuous nonmilitary activity. Another particularly instructive example is that of the 1936 Olympics in Berlin, where the new German chancellor Adolf Hitler pitted his race of so-called supermen against such standard-bearers of the "mongrel" societies as America's gold-medal sprinter Jesse Owens. The whole celebration was actually a prelude to the more obviously military confrontation which began a few years later.

But to say that sports and military activity are uniformly alike in design and intention is too simplistic, because although all sport may be considered a sublimation of aggressive drives, certain games illustrate this better than others, and in fact the manner in which the aggression is sublimated differs greatly from sport to sport. It's much easier to identify the sublimated aggressiveness in modern football, for example, than in a skiing competition. In terms of competitive drives, therefore, we must look at the particular styles in which different sports allow for sublimating aggression and determine what effect each of those styles has on competition.

Now, there are a number of ways to categorize sports. They may be divided into team and individual sports, for example. Or they may be considered in terms of the level of professionalism (or the size of the purse) involved. I will talk about both of these elements later in the chapter. A more useful initial distinction, I think, is a structural one, because the physical arrangement of play has a great bearing on the level and type of competitiveness displayed in any sport: the shape of the field and the arrangement of players on it, in other words, define the degree of competitiveness allowed.

"Side" Sports and "Face" Sports

In terms of the structure of the playing field, most sports can be divided into two major categories: those that are played side by side with the opponent, and those that are played face to face.

In the 1938 movie *Robin Hood,* Errol Flynn is in constant competition with the forces of evil represented by the Sheriff of Nottingham and, more particularly, the wicked Sir Guy, played by

Basil Rathbone. He battles them in a variety of ways, but two scenes from the film come to mind as a way of illustrating the distinction between "side" sports and "face" sports.

In the Nottingham archery contest, Robin is competing with a field of archers, the most promising of whom is the Sheriff's own bowman. After all the others have been eliminated, these two stand together before a target and shoot alternately until Robin emerges the victor. Although the men are using lethal weapons, they are not allowed by the rules to turn those weapons against each other. Nor are they allowed to interfere in any way with the other person's shooting; victory comes to the archer who shoots better without hindering his opponent. Since interference with the rival's performance is specifically prohibited, I would categorize such a contest as a nonhindrance contest.

Thus, archery is a classic example of a "side" sport. The opponents stand side by side and compete without mutual interference for a common goal. In this category fall all those sports which are played, as it were, along parallel lines: races of all types (running, swimming, horse and auto racing, skiing, etc.), golf, shooting, bowling, and such field events as javelin hurling and shot-putting. Except for a few pastimes such as three-legged races, side sports are by definition noncontact sports.

At the end of *Robin Hood,* Flynn and Rathbone engage in a duel to the death which, like the gunfight in Western movies, both crystallizes the real aggression between them and serves as the ultimate competitive test. In this duel they use swords, and battle each other not side by side, but face to face. Robin, of course, wins the competition by killing Sir Guy; what is important to remember here is that he does so not simply by fencing better, but by hindering his opponent from competing to the best of *his* ability. This makes the sword fight a hindrance contest, a typical example of "face" sports.

Unlike side sports, face sports involve a strong defensive element as well as an offensive one. The winner is the person (or team) who not only plays his best but who hinders the opponent from playing his or her best. In this category are found all the various field sports—soccer, football, basketball, volleyball, hockey, tennis, baseball, rugby—as well as such nonfield sports as boxing, wrestling, and the various Eastern martial arts.

One might expect that the face sports would be more competitive than the side sports, but this is an oversimplification of the case. Actually, both can be intensely competitive, as anyone who has watched the faces of Olympic swimmers a couple of minutes before a meet or witnessed the intense rivalry evident among downhill skiers can attest.

The difference between the two types of sport lies, I think, not in the degree of competitiveness involved, but in the degree of permissible aggression. Generally speaking, such Dag tools as physical violence, recklessness, and brute strength can be quite useful to the competitor in a face-to-face sport—provided he or she observes the written and unwritten rules of sportsmanship which are designed to keep the worst kind of aggressiveness in check. The same tools, however, can often be detrimental in a side sport, since it relies much more heavily on the "milder" Dinag tools of perseverance and endurance. Throwing yourself in front of an opposing runner in a foot race, for example, will only get you disqualified. In a football game, it may make you the hero of the play.

Of course, there are limits to the amount of violence that is permitted in even the most violent types of sports. Though the gladiators of ancient times fought to the death (and the more gore the better), the "thirst for blood" that is still evident in today's fans is limited by a whole range of laws and internal regulations.

This is most evident, paradoxically, in those face sports which have evolved along the most violent lines. That is to say, the greater the range of *possible* violence, the greater the number of rules needed to limit and define the *permissible.* There is a kind of internal control mechanism operating in modern contact sports, for example, that simply is not needed in noncontact sports. Tennis has no "unnecessary roughness" rule; professional football would be unthinkable without it.

Tact and Contact

Face sports can be divided into those which allow a good deal of body contact and those which allow very little. The net-style sports (tennis, badminton, ping-pong), although clearly hindrance sports—that is, they require that you interfere with your opponent's progress—are not in any sense contact sports, because the players compete at opposite ends of a court and never do bodily injury to their opponents.

The absence of body contact in a sport does not, of course, ensure the absence of aggressiveness. If you've ever seen Jimmy Con-
nors or Billie Jean King curse themselves and throw their rackets
to the ground after missing a shot, you'll realize that the level of
tension, frustration, and aggression in the big-money tennis tour-
naments can be quite intense. But, as in other net games, the rules
dictate that aggression be channeled into some form other than
physical assaults on opponents. Tennis is a gentleman's game, a
"tact" sport; although it can be played in a direct and aggressive
fashion, the more extreme Dag tools—such as physical violence—
simply are not allowed entrance into the courts.

Such sports as baseball, soccer, hockey, and basketball are
very interesting to watch in terms of competitive styles, because although there are very stringent rules against such Dagish behavior
as roughness and physical assault, the rules obviously are broken
all the time; in fact, the fans—no less than the players—*expect*
them to be broken. The elbow in the ribs, the ball pitched at the
batter's head, the hockey stick jammed into an opponent's legs are
standard procedure in today's professional sports, in spite of the
fact that they regularly put players in the hospital and the penalty
box.

Strictly speaking, hockey is a noncontact sport: there is nothing built into the rules which allows for the kind of aggressive, direct hindrance—the blocking and actual physical attacks—that
characterizes Stanley Cup play. But in contact, as opposed to tact,
sports, it is expected that the rules will be continually "re-
arranged" to allow for the unleashing of the aggressive drives
which attracts many fans to these particular games.

In modern professional football, the level of permissible aggression is so high that elaborate safeguards have had to be fit into
the rules to ensure that the contests do not degenerate into slug-
fests. As I mentioned above, the institution of an "unnecessary
roughness" rule is comprehensible only in the high-hindrance,
high-contact sports in which roughness is part of the very nature
of play. The rules against roughness in boxing and wrestling, for
example, are exact and unwavering because so much aggressiveness is already permitted by the rules that any further infractions
against tact would transform the sport into mere carnage.

There seems, in other words, to be a sort of self-regulatory
process going on in the most aggressively competitive sports. The

more Dagish behavior permitted, the more closely officials must keep an eye out for Dag activity that is out of bounds. Yet it's not surprising that many players seem to become confused by consistently contradictory messages. On the one hand, they are told that the purpose of the game is to knock the other fellow down; on the other, they are told that they must not hurt him in doing so. Surreptitious aggression often arises in cases where the line between *prescribed* and *proscribed* violence has gotten a little fuzzy. To be a successful competitor under such circumstances, the player must make a conscious decision as to whether he will play according to the rules and how many of the Dag tools he will utilize.

This confusion takes an especially complex form when the opponents are not individuals, but teams.

Fouling Out for the Team

During one of the NBA playoff games a few years ago, there were about thirty seconds left of play with the score tied. A New York player had just gone up for a jump shot when an opposing player's arm slashed down, karate style, into his wrist, causing the ball to wobble weakly off court. All the officials immediately called foul, and the shooter, as I recall, ended up making one out of his two free throws, so the opponent's valiant hack ended up being only half successful. And he in turn, having used up his available fouls, was removed from the game.

What is of interest here is that, although the offending player fouled out of the game, his illegal actions had the positive effect of holding New York to a one-point rather than two-point lead: had the shooter sunk the in-play basket, New York would have gotten t͏ ͏o points rather than the one they actually got for the foul shot, and the opposing team would probably have lost any chance of catching up. The player sacrificed himself, in other words, for his team.

We do not normally think of self-sacrifice as a competitive tool. Yet in the context of team effort, it can be a very effective one. In the quest for victory, it is sometimes necessary for one player to accept an individual failure so that his or her team may win, and this suggests not only the enormously complicated nature of collective sports, but also why impermissible violence seems to be so much greater in team sports: hitting below the belt in boxing will very likely make you lose by default, but doing the same thing in football or basketball may get you thrown out of the game while your team, profiting from the foul, can go on to win.

Participation on an athletic team, therefore, frequently changes the entire nature of competitive interaction. A winning team ideally should be the type of organization we described earlier as a positive interdependency group—a structure in which cooperation, rather than individual competitiveness, ensures victory.

Team players learn that individual failure is not so objectionable when it contributes to collective success. They learn, too, that individual success is relatively worthless if it is achieved at the expense of the group. "Superstars" thus can be both an asset and a liability to a team. If they dedicate their skills to an overall effort, they can be invaluable; if not, they can blow the game a lot quicker than the merely competent player who knows how to cooperate. It's not surprising, therefore, that cavalier behavior on the part of star players is generally met with stiff and immediate penalties from their own team: fines, suspension, and so on.

I remember that when I was a child there was a boy named Toby at a summer camp I used to attend. He was without exception the best all-round athlete I had ever encountered. He could hit farther, run faster, stay underwater longer, than any other kid in camp. Yet when it came to team sports, he was a dud. I recall one volleyball game in particular, in which Toby almost ruined our chances for a camp championship by his "superstar" behavior.

Volleyball, a low-hindrance face sport, requires a tremendous amount of collective effort to achieve success. With six people on a side, strategy and cooperation are paramount: the best teams are those which work as a unit, setting up shots for each other, playing combinations rather than attempting to "ace" the ball every time.

Toby couldn't understand this at all. Every time the ball came to him, he would smack it as hard as he could over the net, oblivious of our cries that he pass to one of his teammates in a better position to place the shot. Because Toby was such a good athlete, most of the time his "aces" made the grade, but it wasn't long before the other team realized that, whenever the ball got to him, they could forget about wondering just where it would be returned: it would always be returned by Toby himself. This gave them a competitive edge, and they soon learned to "use" Toby as their own best player. Since they knew he would return everything directly, they simply ganged up on him: all six of their players made all of their returns directly to him, and it wasn't long before he began to tire and make mistakes. Had Toby cooperated with the rest of us, he would have been a real asset to our team, and we would have won easily. As it was, we couldn't make him see that he was blowing the game for everybody, and we finally simply refused to play with him.

There are plenty of Tobys playing sports today, of course, but few of them are ever very successful in team sports. The Tobys of the world are so self-absorbed that they appear to be like auto-compers who do well in individual efforts where cooperation is not a particularly valued competitive tool. When they become members of a team, they are generally millstones around the necks of the other players.

Surrogacy and Fanatics

Modern sport, like the ancient gladiatorial contests, is geared toward the approval and support of vast numbers of spectators. Often this fact has a great effect on the spectators themselves. In many cases today, there is as much competitiveness going on in the stands as on the playing field.

Being observed by others changes the way we act. That is a truism which says a lot about the way many modern competitions are arranged, promoted, and actually played. It is conceivable that the Forest Hills tennis competitions would still be hotbeds of temper and tension even if they were not being filmed nationally. But it is unlikely that Catfish Hunter would have been able to pull down a $5 million salary-and-perquisites package if his fans hadn't flattered him with banners and chants for the previous two seasons. The presence of television and massive audiences at today's sports events has had a great effect on the self-perception of the players. Television allows star athletes to have nationwide followings; in front of the camera competitors who are secure enough to be unaffected by taunts become more rare.

But probably the biggest effect on competitiveness brought about by the new accessibility of sport has been on the fans. Often they are the most aggressive competitors.

On a bus once I overheard a young man discussing a Pittsburgh Steelers-Dallas Cowboys game. He explained to the woman next to him that he was rooting hard for Dallas because, as he put it quite vehemently, "I *hate* Pittsburgh."

Now, this kind of vehemence is by no means uncommon among modern sports fans. Irrational and unfounded as it may be, many fans seem to harbor not only a deep affection for their chosen team, but a rabid and violent hatred for anyone who would dare to oppose them. The rivalry that is set up between the fans of opposing teams can be incredibly intense; when they assert their allegiance to one team or another they are actually competing vicariously. This allows them, when their teams win, to wear the mantle of success without having to prove themselves personally in the field of battle. Thus the teams and the athletes become *surrogates* for many fans who identify with them and yearn to possess their qualities, skills, or competence.

The vicarious honor (or shame) which attaches to a spectator, then, is the principal reason for the popularity of looking at, rather than participating in, sports. Being a fan allows you to compete without really competing. It allows you to release your own aggressive urges by shouting and booing while your surrogate heroes perform the necessary ritual moves on the court or field on your behalf. Some spectators, however, are not content with vicarious competition and act out their own aggression in the stands: the soccer riots which killed dozens of people in Latin America a few years ago are only the most blatant example of how close aggressiveness and "appreciation" can become in the minds of some sports fanatics. A milder example may be perceived in the prevalence of bottle-throwing as a means of showing either appreciation or disdain at baseball games.

Or consider the actions of parents cheering on their Little League sons and daughters. The intensity of the rooting that goes on in such small-time contests is evidence of more than mere parental affection and concern for a child's welfare. When a father reacts with rage as little Johnny blows a grounder, it's probably because he has invested a great deal of his own competitive feelings in his son's activity. He has, in other words, begun to use his child as a surrogate in the same way that he may use Bucky Dent or Reggie Jackson as a surrogate in the field of professional sport.

The same attitude is evident in the behavior of the many bar and club team members who can be found in every tavern and bowling alley across the country. Again, the member of the team—or even the avid supporter—allows the team to satisfy for him something that is not being satisfied elsewhere in his life. By permitting the team to be the surrogate for his own competition, his fears and hopes are projected outward, where perhaps they will be less painful.

Surrogacy in the field of athletics has even taken on a political meaning in recent years. Olympic trials and many other high-level international competitions provide a very good opportunity for people who are not themselves athletes to sublimate not only their physically aggressive drives but even their more cerebral political persuasions into the ostensibly "value-free" arena of sports. The fact that political personages attend the opening games in a baseball season and throw out the first balls is not a mere "tradition" devoid of meaning. It engages public attention—and no politician is averse to this kind of visibility. And the fact that the Palestine Liberation Organization attacked Israel by kidnapping members of its Olympic team at Munich several years ago was not accidental: the games served as a surrogate arena, on which the eyes of the entire world were trained.

Just as some ancient nations pinned their fortunes on a contest between their leading warriors (as, for example, in the case of David and Goliath), so modern nations use the "nonpolitical" metaphor of sport as a means for marshalling patriotic energy and as a way of achieving prestige and success in a geopolitical arena. Not surprisingly (Munich is a vivid example), the use of surrogacy in this way can have extremely violent results.

It is curious that as sports become more violent, we might expect that fans would experience a greater catharsis as spectators and become more subdued from the vicarious working out of turmoils. But this is not happening. In fact, violence seems to be growing in the stands as well as on the field, as if no amount of catharsis is enough—or as if increased violence on the field only whets the fans' appetite for more.

Psychiatrist Arnold Beisser notes, in an interesting article on the psychology of sports fan violence, that fans are actually being taught to expect increased violence:

> With each effort to satisfy their thirst for unexpected violence, their level of tolerance for it increases; thus, they

want more and more. Like someone restricted to a limited
diet, the fan is never completely satisfied, no matter how
violent the contest.*

Thus, there seems to be a law of limited returns built into the psychology of fans who allow players as surrogates to live out their
aggressive competitive fantasies for them. This suggests that the
overall atmosphere of "peanuts, popcorn, and crackerjacks" which
pervades the modern stadium is a mirage; with every new bout of
violence, the frustrated fans demand more.

Rising Stakes

Another factor which has affected the way in which spectators involve themselves in sports is the growth of betting as an adjunct form of participation. It's one thing to pledge your heart and
soul to a team simply because you want your surrogate to go
through the competitive paces for you, but when you have money
riding on Dallas or Ali or the Maple Leafs, your urge to win becomes all the greater. Now you are actually participating through
your investments, not just watching. As the New York City Off
Track Betting ad says, you can "pick a horse and let him run for
you."

From a psychological point of view, betting may be seen as a
way of attempting to buy a team's or a player's loyalty and approval. The hidden dynamic goes something like this: "I think
Walt Frazier is a great guy because he is a better basketball player than I am. So I'm going to put ten dollars down on the next
Knicks game. Then he'll see that I'm a loyal fan and supporter, a
worthy competitor in my own way, and he'll think I'm a great guy
too." Betting thus may become a way of convincing yourself that,
in spite of the fact that you can never hope to compete with your
heroes on their own grounds, you're still doing your part for the
team effort with your own "tools."

This is not the only reason for the rise of betting in sports, of
course. A more obvious one is simply that it makes some people a
great deal of money. Although few of us ever see any of that mon-

* In "The Sports Fan and Recreational Violence," *Psychiatric Annals,* Vol.
9, No. 3 (March 1979), pp. 165–68.

ey, we cherish the hope that some day our number will come up and our bookie will shake loose a few dollars to compensate us for our lifelong support of this boxer or that jockey.

The immense amounts of money involved in modern professional sports have, in fact, radically altered the ways in which spectators and participants alike view the games. What has happened is that sports competition has become monetarized: the small-timers are out, and the big business pros have taken over.

The Business of Sports

There is a thin line in amateur athletics today between purely recreational interest and a kind of semiprofessional intensity. Even when participation is not organized into a league, many amateurs play as if the game were a matter of life or death. This has given rise to a growing number of "weekend jocks" for whom competition is every bit as important as it is to the tennis and golf pros who teach them. People can become quite animated in their efforts to succeed at these weekend enterprises, sometimes as a way of compensating for their failures in other areas.

For a great many so-called amateurs, the notion of the game as fun or recreation has long since disappeared. The deadly competitive spirit present in Little League baseball or Pee Wee hockey games is only one example of the ever-growing trend toward professionalism in amateur sports. Amateur athletics, the mainstay of school sports, have also succumbed to this trend. With the competition for star college athletes so keen, it's inevitable that high school superstars are tapped for top college scholarships, and that professionalism—by which I mean a stress on training and "expertise" at the expense of recreational enjoyment—begins to creep into high school athletics as well.

Beyond college, a hard-bitten attention to competitive gain has more and more taken over: frequently we read about a top athlete, disgruntled with adulation, who claims that baseball—or hockey or tennis—has become "just a job." That is no exaggeration, for when a player is being paid six figures a year to compete, you may be sure that he or she will attach to the game he once considered "fun" the same kind of grim importance most of us place on our livelihoods—for that's just what it has become to him.

With the professionalization of sport has come an ever greater ballyhoo attaching to the end-of-season supergames, to the huge salaries and scholarships given star school athletes, and to the escalating extras given top performers. Competition for athletic excellence is now augmented by competition for pay: the top athlete is not necessarily the one who is the best team player, but the one whom the fans pay to see, the madcap or the notoriously eccentric star. And, as the superstars' salaries grow, the very nature of the team effort is undermined. Sports become yet another business or industry. As the clubhouse system gives way to the free-agent system, this competition is both codified and intensified.

It's difficult to imagine Joe DiMaggio letting himself be bought out by another team in the heyday of the old Yankees. Today that kind of team loyalty is giving way to the search for bigger and better contracts: baseball players especially find themselves jaunting around the country like peripatetic businessmen, in search of the pot of gold.

Another effect of the evolution of the surrogate star system has been increasing *specialization:* the introduction since World War II of the professional place kicker and the professional base stealer indicates the importance of using not completely well-rounded athletes, but men and women who have focused all their energies on perfecting a single necessary skill and who serve the purpose of having special appeal for a certain segment of the fan population. The star system, with its big business attitude, thus has led to a situation where the very nature of the sports themselves has changed. What effect all this may have on the players' competitive performances is difficult to gauge. Probably Catfish Hunter plays no worse at a salary of one million a year than he did at fifty thousand, but the common assumption is that he plays better—and that assumption is, at best, suspect.

Recreational Sports: Is the Game Still a Game?

While amateur athletics have been turning more and more toward professional standards, what has been happening to recreational sports? Aren't most of us, after all, competing on the playing field just for the fun of it? What is the competitive difference between recreational sport and amateur athletic activity?

Recreational activity is done for enjoyment. I participate in a sport because it makes me feel good. Depending on my own competitive makeup, I can set my own pace. As an autocomper I can run as far or as fast as I wish, attempting to better only my own individual performance. I can play without worrying about who wins and who loses. The psychological benefit of being able to perform a sport well is in my enhanced sense of physical and emotional well-being.

When I have a patient in treatment, regardless of what his or her particular problem is, I know that the patient has turned the corner and is on the road to recovery when he or she starts to participate in recreational athletic activity. My most disturbed patients are unable to mobilize their own internal physical and psychological resources in order to do this. Once they are feeling better about themselves, however, the mere fact of participation begins to improve their self-concept and self-image, which in turn furthers their recovery.

Recreational athletics can involve either individual or group competition with others or autocompetition. The tools and methods used by each participant will be consonant with his or her overall competitive style. With those who have competitive problems, recreational athletic activity can become a difficult area, while for those who are comfortable with their own prowess and do not feel the need to prove this to others, it can provide all the things which our earliest childhood athletic activities offer the young child: health, education, and enjoyment.

Wanda Collins, whom we met at the beginning of the book, is a case in point. She is not a very good tennis player, but she doesn't mind playing without winning, because she has learned to enjoy the game for its own sake. A Dinagish competitor, she has mastered the art of "no-win winning" and plays for the sheer enjoyment of it.

Danny Marchant, on the other hand, loses on the court no matter what the score, because he takes his "recreation" so seriously that he cannot possibly have any fun while playing. When he plays with Perry Stiles, for example, he's out for blood; even when he wins he feels he should have won by a greater margin. The difference between them is in their attitudes—Perry never feels as though he has lost to Danny and Danny can't stand this. A former captain of the Harvard tennis team, Perry is an excellent tennis player. So is Danny, but his motivation to beat Perry, which stems from his sibling rivalry with Barbara, is so intense that whenever he loses, he becomes very upset and occasionally even develops migraine headaches. Danny has distorted "recreation" into self-punishment. The worst aspect of this is that when Danny wins, since Perry doesn't suffer in defeat, it is no victory for Danny.

There has been a marked increase in recreational athletic activity during the 1970s. This is due partially to the increased leisure and affluence of our society and also to our increasing recognition of the physical and psychological benefits afforded by participation in sports. Most of this recreational activity takes the form of autocomps, with running the prime example. Although an increasing number of runners have decided to enter marathons, most of the estimated 25 million runners in the United States are participating at their own pace and for their own self-enrichment. This is really the whole point of recreational athletics.

There are dangers, however. Some people become so psychologically dependent on the sense of well-being they achieve from recreational sports that they overextend themselves. Medical journals have recently started to report increasing numbers of recreational athletes who injure themselves and yet continue to participate until they cause themselves some real physical problems. Unfortunately, then, the autocomper can often self-destruct. When the recreational athlete starts to assume this compulsive posture, he is beginning to resemble the amateur athlete who aspires to become a professional. In such cases, winning assumes an importance that is inappropriate for purely recreational sports.

Is Winning Everything?

We have seen that as the stakes of playing sports rise dramatically, the recreational aspects of the game fall away and are replaced by a dedication to victory at all costs. Whether the game is played on the amateur or the professional level, how you play automatically takes a back seat to winning per se, and in the pursuit of that goal sportsmanlike conduct gives way to increasing levels of direct and intense aggression.

What effect does this have on competitive behavior? I would speculate that, first of all, it increases the likelihood of cheating and the use of officially prohibited competitive tools to ensure winning. Such varied techniques as drug injections, psychological harassment of the opposing players, and actual physical assaults in pile-ups all point to the ease with which, in a world where winning means everything, tact can give way to attack.

Secondly, it increases the potential level of anxiety and stress on the part of all concerned. Losing a Little League game when their parents are watching in the stands creates a good deal of anxiety for young players; losing a World Series when the stakes are not parental approval but a large monetary bonus for each player is bound to create a level of tension that is enormous compared to that generated by purely recreational activity.

And thirdly, it invites confusion about goals and values. It tends to cut down on the variety of styles the players are allowed to adopt, and makes the players not only directly aggressive, but to some extent Bullies.

Convinced that the "Winning is All" philosophy has severely damaged certain aspects of sport, some fans have begun to devise ways of encouraging people to participate in athletics cooperatively rather than competitively. Chief among the proponents of this new approach to sport has been the New Games Foundation, established in San Francisco in 1973. Its members strive to create "no-win" games such as Vampire Blob, in which anyone "bitten" on the neck by another player joins that player as part of a collective "monster." The goal in such games is to teach the virtues of cooperation and innocent fun which most of our games today assiduously deny.

A "Tug-of-Peace" designed by Canadian psychologist Terry Orlick, for example, shows what a little imagination can do to modify the winner-loser syndrome. Orlick proposes that players, rather than competing team against team, pull on an assemblage of ropes to create designs cooperatively. This would retain the physical benefits of tug-of-war games, while redefining the nature of the game so that it is seen not as a substitute for battle, but as a delight in community creativity. "The point," Orlick was quoted as saying in *Time* magazine, "is to have fun interacting, not to put someone else down."

Critics claim that such noncompetitive games are bound to unleash aggressive drives into less safe and less organized outlets. They also say that games predicated on the "sameness"—rather than on the competitive "differentness"—of the participants are unrealistic. And there is at least a reasonable suspicion in my own mind that those who claim to be cooperating rather than competing in these games are really only competing in more subtle ways: they may, for example, be striving with each other for a general group approval rather than for the accolades of outsiders. Thus one may find the spirit of competition everywhere—even in an avowedly anticompetitive activity!

Nevertheless, proponents of the games have found them to promote the development of positive self-concepts in many participants, since they establish situations in which everyone "wins" rather than just a few. While "no win" games as such will probably never entirely replace "win" games, they may ultimately provide a good balance to certain types of excessively aggressive competition. Imagine, for example, what the fate of Woody Hayes (the Ohio State University football coach who lost his job for punching an opposing player) might have been had he been trained early in his career in the intricacies of "Tug-of-Peace." It might have been, as the pundits say, a whole new ball game.

Competitive sport, then, frequently serves as both a sublimation of and a metaphor for basic aggressive drives. It begins to serve in this double manner from the moment children begin playing games, although it seems to make its first clear-cut appearance as a sublimating factor in adolescence, when the child's physical capacities expand in ways that often are best managed through strenuous activity.

The physical transformations of adolescence, however, cannot be wholly managed by involvement in sports. Puberty leads to an interest in various other kinds of physical activities as well, chief among them being sexual activity. Sex has been called the most popular of indoor sports. As we shall see in the next chapter, it can be every bit as competitive as games played out of doors.

BATTLE OF THE SEXES:
Competition in the Bedroom

Several years ago a middle-aged couple with three teenaged daughters came to me for consultation about the youngest of the three. Lisa was fourteen at the time, and in the past year, they explained, she had become increasingly defiant and uncooperative, both at home and at school. Her attendance record was poor, and even when she did attend classes, the teachers could not manage to interest her in her work. At home she was sullen and nasty to her older sisters. The parents were at a loss.

I met with Lisa alone for the first time a couple of days later. It didn't take long to discover that her parents' description had been fairly accurate. She confessed to me her hostility toward her sisters, and acknowledged readily that she was simply not interested in school. It was a fairly standard case of sibling rivalry in which the younger sibling, overshadowed by the older and more "attractive" ones, felt herself rejected and unwanted by her parents. Her parents did little to correct this impression, since they were both quite busy with business and community affairs, and couldn't seem to find the time to spend with any of their daughters that the children obviously needed. Their lack of attention to Lisa aggravated her feelings of inferiority, and so it wasn't long before she began cutting classes and "acting up" to attract their attention.

But the most interesting fact I discovered in talking to Lisa was that, in addition to rebelling against her parents' inattention by becoming disobedient, she was also extremely active sexually: within the past year, she told me, she had been to bed with over a dozen boys. She was, in fact, beginning to develop a "reputation" at school; the fact that her parents did not know this was an indication of their lack of awareness and sensitivity to her.

It was obvious that Lisa's promiscuity was provoked by her feelings of inferiority in relation to her sisters and by feeling unwanted by her parents. She had entered high school with grades that were not quite up to those of her siblings, and she had just about begun to resign herself to being "second best" there, as she had been in grammar school, when she discovered a startling fact: if she went to bed with boys, *they* would like her; if only for a while, *they* would give her the attention that her family would not give her.

So, Lisa adopted sex as a prime competitive tool. It had a salutary double effect: first, it was a way of punishing her inattentive parents by flouting their own sexual standards; and second, it got back at her sisters by making Lisa successful in a field in which they had not even begun to experiment. As soon as Lisa discovered that she could secure the image, if not the substance, of affection from her liaisons, she started using sex quite indiscriminately, gradually changing it from a mere *tool* into her entire *field* or arena of competitive behavior. Since she could not compete on the home front, she switched arenas, and in her new chosen field (sexuality), she perceived herself, for the first time in her life, as a success.

However, she wasn't genuinely happy about herself. For one thing, she had changed arenas, so she was not really competing well with her sisters. Also, she was smart enough to know the difference between honest affection and attention paid to someone for the purposes of gaining sexual favors. The more boys she ended up with in bed, the more she began to see that, while this might have been better than no attention at all, it was really not what she wanted. Sexually, she was a good competitor, but she had chosen the wrong arena to fulfill herself. Inside she still felt like a failure; that, in fact, was one of the reasons she had to change boyfriends continually: she needed constant proof that she was desirable.

Fortunately, Lisa came into therapy while she was still young enough to reverse her dysfunctional behavior pattern. Through conjoint sessions with her parents, we were able to help the family become aware of how they were failing to meet Lisa's needs. They then began to interact with her more meaningfully, and eventually, as she started to feel better about herself, she became more interested in school, learned to compete with her peers in less self-destructive ways, and ultimately settled down with one boyfriend.

Lisa's story illustrates only one of the many patterns in which that popular center-box tool, sex, can be used in a competitive manner and even transformed, unfortunately, into a person's major competitive arena. Promiscuity is a fairly common human response to the felt need for approval and affection, and since our society has made it very easy to confuse sexual contact with affection, people like Lisa (both male and female) adopt it frequently as a way of getting the attention they need. Like the wide variety of games on the playing field, there are many sexual games or patterns which are no less common; in this chapter we'll see how some of them operate, and discover how they can often frustrate rather than really satisfy the need for approval.

Lisa's use of sex falls into the category of behavior which I call genital competition: the use of actual physical sexuality in a competitive manner. This type of behavior arises often in the early teenage years: puberty naturally focuses a good deal of attention on sex as a new pleasure, as forbidden fruit, and also as a competitive tool. Before puberty, sex is already used as a competitive tool. But the kinds of ways in which it is used by preadolescent children are basically not genital as yet. We start competing sexually with members of the opposite sex well before we know what "sex" is all about, and we do so in behavior patterns that fall into the category I call gender competition.

No Girls Allowed

There's a humorous drawing which used to find its way onto posters and greeting cards a few years back. It showed a little boy and a little girl looking down into each other's underpants, with the caption, "There *is* a difference!" Although this does not appear to be a competitive act, comparison is frequently central to competition. Moreover, as harmless and amusing as this image might have seemed to an adult, it does suggest something not entirely heartening about the onset of sexual competition between the sexes.

The recognition of the simple physical difference between boys and girls is, for a child, one of the truly amazing discoveries of his or her early years. The kind of revelation suggested by the drawing is a commonplace of childhood, as children continually "explore" the mysteries of the opposite sex in games such as "Playing House" and "Doctor." There is nothing unnatural about this; on the contrary, it would be strange if Johnny were not aware that Mary had a vagina but no penis, or if she didn't notice that the reverse was true for him. Yet, partly because of the children's own confusion about their differentness and partly because of the way in which our culture handles this issue, the recognition of genital differences often leads to unhealthy competitive behavior between boys and girls.

Very early, the recognition of purely physical differences is ingested and then forgotten, after which children, like their elders before them, begin to invent a host of nonphysical distinctions based on the forgotten physical one. These distinctions, in turn, form the basis for the competitive interactions between the sexes which I have termed gender, rather than genital, competition.

Gender competition, as I define it here, is competition between members of the opposite sex which is not based, or not perceived as based, on the simple physical differences between them. Gender competition begins shortly after boys and girls have understood that girls can make babies and boys can urinate standing up. With the onset of puberty, it begins to take some curious new twists, as an intensification of the interest in physical differentness (this time with a new motivation) adds genital competition to the already established gender competition, to produce a far more complicated set of battle lines than before. This pattern continues, with modifications, into adulthood, although by then it is frequently compounded by various types of genital competition. The "battle of the sexes" has its origin in gender competition.

It is important to note that the physical difference which forms the basis for intersexual rivalry is seldom acknowledged by those engaging in it. The group of little girls who refuse to let Johnny play house with them are not likely to hang a sign on the outside of their room announcing "No Penises Allowed." And the boy who refuses to play ball with Mary because she is "just a girl" doesn't say either aloud or to himself, "I wish *I* could make a baby." But the genital distinction is, however surreptitiously, remembered; and it gives rise to much of the other competition between the sexes both in the formative years and later.

The physical distinctions between boys and girls are not merely genital ones. Generally, girls mature physically a little earlier than boys, and this provides an additional cause for the beginnings of gender competition. That is, as girls begin to develop athletically a little ahead of the boys, Johnny adopts the "just a girl" taunt as a way of disguising the fact that he cannot compete with Mary to his own satisfaction. Rather than using a Dag tool, in other words, he adopts the Indagish tool of cunning and comes up with a plan whereby he will not *have* to compete with her in a footrace: the footrace is "for boys only."

To the extent that parents adhere to or themselves fulfill traditional sex-role stereotypes, boy-girl differences and the segregation of the sexes are further reinforced. Parents who support these stereotypical norms of behavior also set up expectations for their children to behave in ways which accentuate sex-role differences. As the children fulfill these expectations, they begin to believe that girls are "inferior" to boys and should not participate in "tomboyish" activities.

Thus gender competition may be a way originally for the less physically competent male to win against the more competent female simply by adjusting the rules. This may save his pride for a while, but it obviously has some serious social consequences, not the least of which is the resentment of girls (and later women) that they have been arbitrarily excluded from certain areas because they were either a) capable of becoming pregnant or b) capable of beating Johnny in a footrace.

The humorous early aspects of the battle of the sexes, then, may be seen as prototypical of the way men and women relate to each other later in life—though as time goes on the battle may grow less and less amusing. Think, for example, of the women's movement. Could it not be seen in part as an ultimate extension of gender competition, in which the "little girls" are finally demanding of the "little boys" that the clubhouse doors be opened? A frequent male response to the gender competitive strivings of the

women's movement is to attempt to sexualize and therefore deni-
grate the women's performance by responding on the level of genital competition.

Anything You Can Do . . .

In *A Moveable Feast,* Ernest Hemingway relates a poignant
incident regarding his friend F. Scott Fitzgerald which illustrates
very well the way in which gender competition can drift over into
genital competition.

Fitzgerald—then living in Paris—was "blocked" in the middle of a novel, and after some hedging and embarrassment he confessed to his fellow writer that he had been unable to work for
weeks because his wife, Zelda, had been criticizing him constantly,
trying to prove that she was every bit as much a "creative genius"
as he was. Recently she had even begun to ridicule his sexual
prowess and masculinity; his measurements were such that he
could never satisfy a woman, she alleged. The accusation was
bothering him so much that he had been unable to get anything
down on paper.

Hemingway took his distraught friend by the arm and led
him to the WC. After a look at Fitzgerald's penis, Hemingway assured him that all was in order. Fitzgerald still wasn't convinced,
so Hemingway led him to the Louvre, where they spent some time
strolling through galleries of ancient male nude statues. Fitzgerald's self-doubts started to fade, as Hemingway knew they would,
when he saw that his "equipment" was just as good as any other
man's.

Now, whether or not that cleared up Scott and Zelda's sexual
problems is open to question—sexual incompatibility is obviously
more a function of attitude and communication than of genital en-
dowment. Because of Zelda's emotional instability there were other problems in the relationship also. But what I wish to stress in
citing this incident is the use of sexuality as a competitive tool, and
the way genital competition can often augment, indeed confuse, an
original gender rivalry.

Zelda, clearly, felt extremely jealous of men in general and of
her husband in particular. A writer herself, and a good one, she
felt overpowered by Scott's success and ongoing creative work;
their gender competition had had a long and complicated career.

But when she felt, apparently, that she was finally losing that competition entirely, she pulled out a competitive tool which she knew would be bound to restore the balance: sexual intimidation. Perceiving herself to be failing as a writer vis-à-vis her husband, she adopted the role of the Ball-Buster and implied that, since Scott was no good in bed, he wasn't much good anywhere else either. The incident thus supplies a vivid example of how the implication of *genital* inferiority can be used as an effective tool in the competition for *gender* supremacy.

The Fitzgerald case is an example of competitive resentment on the part of a frustrated woman leading to a change of competitive arena and the adoption of a new competitive tactic. You'll notice the similarity between Zelda's maneuver and that of Lisa, who also shifted tools and arenas to assert her superiority over others.

Of course, it's not only women who do this. Men are clearly as culpable when it comes to using sexual intimidation as a tool to get what they want. Zelda no doubt was reacting in part to what she perceived as Scott's greater dedication to his career than to her (which in fact was not true), and she used sexual insult as a way, among other things, to recapture his attention. Men do this all the time with women they perceive to be "unresponsive" to their sexual advances. How many times have you heard a man who has failed to "score" with a woman (an interesting metaphor brought to the sexual arena from the playing field) explain away his lack of success by describing her as "frigid," or a "prude" or a "bitch"? Such sexual insults, whether or not they are directed to the woman in person, are tools employed by men who need reassurance that they are still desirable and that something else—that is, the woman—caused their "failure" in this particular case. For every Ball-Buster, in other words, there is an overgrown Brastrap-Snapper who reacts to rejection with a time-honored competitive technique: insult, and specifically sexual insult. In the battle of the sexes, you must remember, sexuality can be used, and very often is used, as an offensive, retaliatory tactic. It can be used gently, affectionately, as a way of securing responsiveness; but that is by no means the only, or even the dominant, modality. Sex is just as often used as punishment—as a way of saying "I'm doing better than you"—as it is as a way of sharing warmth.

The highly competitive nature of modern life has, not surprisingly, invaded our sexual lives as well. We live in a world in which sexuality is used to sell everything from cigarettes to soap to soft drinks, in which the traditional monogamistic mores have broken down and where "swinging" is taken by many people to be the most desirable form of sexual behavior. Competition for and around sex—competition to see who can have the "most" sex or the "best" sex—is keen. Thus, in a world in which sexuality is as fluid as it is today, genital competition becomes the rule rather than the exception.

The examples I have mentioned so far are of behavior that took place between members of the opposite sex. A great deal of genital competition, however, goes on not between the sexes but between members of the same sex. That is, there is a great deal of genital competition in our culture which does not have a gender component.

Lisa, for example, was not competing *with* boys, but *for* them. Her competitors were her two sisters and, by extension, all the other girls in her peer group. The promiscuity which Lisa's case illustrates is one element of genital competition among both boys and girls of high school age—although clearly that kind of behavior, in today's Playboy culture, does not stop after high school. What Lisa was unconsciously saying to herself was, "I can't compete with my sisters on their own grounds. So I'll change the arena and use sex to get ahead of them. I'll show them who's really more desirable."

Lisa carried her quest for sexual approval to an extreme. Not all adolescents go that far: most are content to keep their genital competition at a spoken, and unacted, level. Both boys and girls in high school locker rooms, for example, are given to making comparisons between their own "equipment" and that of their peers. The rather childish expression "Mine is bigger than yours" may be taken as a kind of catchphrase of adolescent sexual competition. At a time when young people are just becoming aware of their sexuality, simple comparisons of this sort are often a major part of the competition.

Boasting also plays a part—whether or not the claims can be verified. I recall a high school classmate named Tony who had "matured," or so he liked to think, a little earlier than the rest of us. Every Monday during lunch, while the rest of us traded tales of the amusement parks we had visited or the fishing trips we had taken over the weekend, Tony would regale us with stories of how many new sexual "positions" he and his girlfriend had thought up and tried out while we were playing kids' games.

Tony was adept at using a Dag tool—boasting—to lord it over us in the field of genital competition. It wasn't until years later, when I was able to think about him from a psychological perspective, that I could see he was engaging in what I call compensatory sexual competition. He came from a miserable home situation, I remembered; his father beat him with some frequency. In addition, he was not very good academically. So for Tony as for Lisa, sexual prowess had increased significance: it served to compensate for his perceived failure in other areas.

This kind of behavior pattern, although it often begins in high school, is quite common as well among adults who confuse sexual "accomplishment" with personal, psychological success. The modern sexual revolution has only heightened the confusion about this issue and given rise to an army of "liberated" Don Juans, Casanovas, and Studs. Their presence suggests one of the most widespread problems concerning genital competition, one which is continually reinforced by television, movies, and even modern literature: the confusion of promiscuity with freedom.

I Can't Get No Satisfaction

Roberta was an attractive, intelligent twenty-six-year-old woman who came to me complaining that, although she was dating frequently, she couldn't seem to get involved with a man past the initial sexual encounter.

"I don't know what's wrong with me," she said. "Every time I get into a relationship with a guy I get angry at him."

"What do you do?" I asked.

"After we've made love, I feel disgusted with him. I get really critical and tell him he's no good as a lover."

During treatment Roberta revealed that she had come from a family headed by a career military officer who was extremely rigid and strict in his demands for discipline. She had grown up watching her mother being berated by her father because she was unable to live up to his standards, and Roberta herself had often been the target of his oppression and abuse. She learned to hate him for his insensitivity, and later extended that hatred to demanding men in general.

In terms of competitive success, this had both a positive and a negative effect. The positive effect was that Roberta became intensely competitive in school, assuming a Dagish stance as a way of showing the boys that, unlike her father, they could not abuse her, and that she would become more successful than they; a rather unhappy motivation, perhaps, but it gained her numerous academic honors, and a job in one of the country's most prestigious engineering firms after graduation.

The negative effect was that, in using her own sexuality as a weapon against men, Roberta ensured that she would be unable to have a decent relationship with any of her many dates. Unconsciously identifying her father with most men made her abuse them sexually just as he had abused her and her mother. In terms of actual lovemaking, Roberta insisted on taking the superior position at all times; she could not allow herself to have an orgasm for fear that this would indicate she was losing control, letting down her defenses. So, she went from bed to bed, seeking in vain for the relationship which her own aggressive behavior sabotaged.

Luckily for Roberta, she sought help in time to make her realize the underlying causes for her bed-hopping; with treatment she eventually came to understand how she had been chained to the events in her past, and she was able to learn to relax and to start to enjoy sex, to "experiment" with softness as well as control.

Many Bed-Hoppers are not so lucky. The common image of the Don Juan, for example, is that of a happy-go-lucky fellow who is so adept at, and so fond of, sex that he sleeps with a different woman every night and never gets tired or bored. The inner reality, however, may be far from this charming picture.

Psychologist Otto Rank, in his *Don Juan Legend,* suggests that the famed lover's search for the Ideal Woman may be a metaphor for his need to recapture the affection and security of his earliest days—that the Ideal Woman, in other words, is in reality the mother he has long ago lost and can never regain. This is an illuminating way of looking at Don Juan and all other Bed-Hoppers. What it suggests is that, far from being utterly content with their freewheeling life-styles, they may be desperate for an assurance which never comes, and they may be using sexual conquests, as my friend Tony used boasting, to disguise the fact that they never find satisfaction. This is similar to the way in which the goal-vaulting autocomper becomes so caught up in the process of competing (of searching for the lost mother in this case) that he cannot take the time to appreciate the goal once it is achieved.

The same pattern operates in many adulterous relationships. Among single people, promiscuity may indicate simply an unmet need for assurance. Among married people, it is often a sign of competitive dissension within the marriage.

Consider the case of Martin and Joan Blakely from our cocktail party as an example. A dual-career couple without children, they experienced something which is increasingly common among such couples: divorce brought about by the inability to balance the competitive needs of the partners. Throughout their marriage, gender competition had been intense, and Joan had worked her way up in an advertising agency to become a successful account executive in her attempt to compete with Martin. Martin, after about five years, started to feel not an equal partner but an adjunct to his wife. She made more money than he did, she was more widely known, she was constantly on the move; although he enjoyed his own career, it was not as exciting as hers. He began to feel in her shadow, and to feel stuck always two steps behind her. She became a more colorful Indagish competitor while he felt like a lackluster Dinag.

In this state of mind, he fell into first one, then a series of affairs, utilizing Indag tools with which he was not totally comfortable, such as guile and deceit. Realizing (or believing) that he could not compete with Joan within the marriage, he decided to try his hand at competing outside. The more successful she became, the more he began to wonder whether or not he was "man enough" for her; and in fact their sexual life together, increasingly on the wane, only nourished his doubts. When Joan withdrew from him sexually—refusing to compete in that area at all—he charged her with being "hung up"; she countered by calling him "oversexed." Eventually, he responded to her taunt by having extramarital affairs.

The affairs were a way of assuring Martin that he was sexually, and competitively, all right. But he could not conceal them from Joan—indeed, he made sure she found out about them by being "spotted" on a date by friends, as a way of getting back at his wife. The issue tore the marriage apart.

The search for sexual satisfaction, then, very seldom is confined to the search for a gratifying physical experience. Almost always gender and genital competition play a part; but seeing your-self as a failure in those areas of competition virtually ensures that, no matter how many partners you may have, you will regard yourself as a sexual failure as well.

I'm Not in the Mood

Of course, many sexual problems do have an immediate phys-ical component. The growing popularity of sexual dysfunction treatment programs is evidence both that the symptoms of sexual maladjustment are widespread and that treatment has become ac-ceptable: people do not come to be treated for the underlying cause so much as the resulting effect.

What are some of the effects of sexual imbalance between partners?

As I've implied in the last section, many sexual difficulties can appear to be not difficulties at all, but strengths. Don Juan-ism, which has a clearly neurotic basis, is seen in our culture as a vaunted achievement; you can never (so goes the current belief) get too much sex.

Too little is another matter, though. Generally, the sexual problems a psychiatrist sees are those of deficiency rather than ex-cess. These are more clearly recognized as real problems that may also be tied up with gender and genital competition.

Frigidity, for example, as well as impotence is associated with competitive dysfunctions. Both types of failure may be used as a way of withdrawing approval from a partner who is seen as com-petitively "one up"; both may result from a competitive emphasis on "performance" rather than relaxation in the sexual act.

Phil, referred to me by his family doctor because he had be-gun to suffer from impotence, was married to Mary Ann, a quiet, unassertive, Indinagish woman. They got along well as long as Mary Ann did not make any demands on him. Whenever she as-sumed the dominant or aggressive role in their sexual relationship, however, Phil immediately became impotent.

In treatment Phil revealed that he was the youngest son of a demanding, intrusive mother and an uninvolved, distant father. His two older sisters, whom his mother seemed to favor, also at-tempted to boss Phil. All three of these women were essentially Dagish and castrating. As Phil grew up, he came to hate his mother and his sisters for the continual, critical directions they gave him.

As a result, Phil developed exceedingly ambivalent feelings about all women. Although he was attracted to them and started to date frequently in his final years of high school and in college, he was turned off as soon as a woman required something of him. Usually the woman didn't start placing demands on him until she had grown to know him somewhat, so that he was able to date for a short period of time without any difficulty. After college, when he took a job in industry, he noticed that he could get along with the women in his section until they started asking him to do them favors or to work for them. An Indagish person himself, he would become hostile and aggressive toward them as a defense.

The pattern, of course, repeated itself with Mary Ann. Initially, Phil was attracted to her because of her reserved manner. When Mary Ann became more relaxed with Phil and started to become more assertive, he grew very resistant and unresponsive. And the more sexually aggressive she became, the more difficulty he had in performing. In effect, since he was angry with her for changing, he subconsciously did not wish to satisfy her. He took revenge by periodically losing his erection. This, however, angered and humiliated him, and he began blaming his wife for his sexual difficulties. It got so bad that Mary Ann was afraid to have sex with Phil because she feared the consequences. At this point, she convinced him that he should seek professional help.

I used a combination of individual and couples therapy to help Phil and Mary Ann resolve their sexual difficulties. I also relied on the "sensate focus" exercises developed by Masters and Johnson, which are designed to teach couples to relax during love-making rather than feeling pressured by demands, either spoken or imagined, for "performance." Before long they had begun to relate to each other better, Phil's impotence had disappeared, and he was dealing better too with the women in his office.

Phil's case indicates what can happen when a person who is used to winning the gender competition battle is suddenly confronted with a genital test which he or she perceives as insurmountable. Phil was used to dominating Mary Ann, and he interpreted her increasingly overt advances to him in the bedroom not as reachings-out, but as threats to his dominance. His response was to retreat from the field altogether, to refuse to compete in a way to which he was unaccustomed. This had the double effect of allowing him to feel *above* the competition, and of putting Mary Ann, who was pushing for a superior position, one step down again. Neither effect, of course, was doing Phil or the relationship any good.

Total impotence or frigidity are not widespread, but a less direct type of withdrawal is fairly common. By this I mean the response that "I'm just not up to it tonight" or "I'm just not in the mood." This response, which has become a cliché in popular literature, actually indicates in many cases the same kind of competitive refusal to play the sexual games that frank impotence and frigidity do.

Let's take the case of Dick and Harriet next. Both were high school teachers in the same school system. Although their subjects were different, they experienced a good deal of gender competition regarding their jobs, as first Harriet and then Dick started spending extra time at school activities and less time with each other at home in order to prove themselves superior.

Dick became so involved in his activities that he began to see them as more important, on a day-to-day basis, than his wife. Eventually, he did not have time even to make love to Harriet, and when she complained of his lack of attention, he explained that he was just too tired after a strenuous day at work. When they did have intercourse, he suffered from premature ejaculation. Psychologically, he was getting sex over with in a hurry so as not to give her too much pleasure.

I involved Dick and Harriet in "couple crisis intervention" therapy, a form of brief treatment that seemed appropriate for their difficulties. Within a couple of months, they were able to see that each of them had contributed to Dick's "tiredness" and "quick trigger," and that if his sexual interest in Harriet and his ability to perform were to be restored, they would both have to make an effort to focus attention on each other as well as on their outside careers. Time, I explained, is not limited when it comes to affectionate response; what they had been missing was not the time to deal with each other, but the will.

Performance

One of the most common difficulties associated with sexuality today is the failure of one partner to "perform" sexually to the satisfaction or expectation of the other. The new sexual freedom is placing increasing demands for performance on all of us; as a result, we are seeing a greater emphasis on competition in the sexual area. As the media have intensified their emphasis on open and relaxed sexuality and sexual mores, each one of us experiences mounting internal pressures and tensions to start changing our attitudes and actions in light of these new norms. I have heard many young people complaining of the pressures they experience to increase their sexual activity. They feel that in order to be accepted, to compete with their peers, they must do things that they might not do under other circumstances. These increased sexual pressures—and older adults are experiencing them as well these days—can be quite severe, leading to a good deal of anxiety over "performance."

Roger and Millie, for example, came to me for couples therapy because their marriage was in a state of turmoil. Roger had started to press his wife to get involved in group sex, telling her that their sex life had become dull and uninteresting. As I got to know him, it became clear that Roger was doing this in an attempt to validate his own poor sense of masculinity. Millie could not tolerate the thought of group sex, and initially had resisted his demands, but as Roger continued to demand that they get involved in "swinging," she allowed herself to be forced into a situation where they swapped partners with a couple they had recently met. Naively, she thought that this might help save their marriage.

The experience did not work out well for either of them, and after it occurred Millie convinced Roger that they should seek professional help.

In a sense, Roger was forcing Millie to compete with other women to prove that *he* was sexually adequate. When she had refused to compete in the sexual arena, Roger's feelings of inadequacy were intensified. By forcing her to participate, Roger felt more "masculine" and in control of their relationship.

When I first saw them, Millie was very angry. She felt betrayed and coerced. Since Roger had forced her into this action, she felt that he could neither love nor respect her. For his part, Roger found that he was not the great Casanova he had hoped he would be. The experiment in "swapping" had, ironically, only intensified his feelings of masculine inadequacy. The situation nearly heralded the death of the marriage.

Fortunately, because Roger had "bombed out" that night, he

was willing to take a look at what was going on in his individual life. Because Millie genuinely loved him and wanted to stay married, she was willing to help him in conjoint sessions to work through some of his long-standing feelings of inadequacy and disappointment. She was also willing to make some changes in her own sexual functioning in order to accommodate Roger. This succeeded in bringing some of the "spice" back into their sexual life. Thus they were able to salvage their marriage, and they reverted to less mutually destructive forms of competition.

Not only have the relaxed sexual mores of this generation led to pressure on individuals to engage in types of sexual activity condemned in earlier periods, but there has been a steadily increasing focus on performance as a goal of lovemaking. This can lead to a quantitative rather than qualitative appraisal of sex, with results that are both ludicrous and quite harmful for everyone involved. We have all heard the amusing tales of the all-night lovers who judge their sexual performance on the basis of how many times they have achieved orgasm, or have helped their partners to achieve orgasm. Such an attitude can be psychologically damaging, because it detracts from the pleasure of the moment which is one of the real delights of sex: if your attention is all devoted to counting up orgasms, it's unlikely you're going to have a very good time on the way. And, in many of the cases I have seen, a concern for "getting there" at a specified time or speed leads to the common dysfunction of premature ejaculation for the man and resultant dissatisfaction for the woman.

In other words, a "Winning is Everything" attitude toward sexuality is no more effective in creating real victory in the bedroom than it is on the playing field. In sex far more than in almost any other endeavor, playing the game for the sheer fun of it is far more important, in terms of final satisfaction for all concerned, than toting up heavy scores. I have already spoken of how Don Juanism may be seen as a hallmark of the dissatisfied rather than satisfied lover; the same is true of the inveterate All-Night Lover.

The Two Revolutions

The undue stress on performance has been both aggravated and alleviated by the sexual revolutions of our day. Or rather, it has been aggravated by one and somewhat helped by the other.

The first revolution, commonly called the sexual (genital) revolution, started around the mid-1950s, and paralleled the rise of *Playboy* magazine and its attendant clubs. While it is clear that the liberalization which began in those years helped many people to appreciate their sexuality more directly, it also had a deleterious effect on many young people who could not cope well with the new demands being made on them by peers who had begun bed-hopping. That is to say, the sexual revolution intensified genital competition, both between the sexes and between members of the same sex. And this made it much harder than ever to reconcile the universal human need for real affection with the new zeal for sexual experience.

Girls who refused to "come across" were considered "square" or "prudes." Boys who could not "score" were considered sexual failures. As the case of Lisa showed, a kind of surrogate affection could be secured simply by "putting out," although genuine emotional needs remained unfulfilled.

The sexual, or genital, revolution is now recognized as having fostered nearly as many problems as it has solved. In ushering in a more flexible morality, it increased the possibilities for genital competition enormously. But for many who never reach the fantasied level of excellence, it is psychologically quite damaging. The character played by Diane Keaton in Woody Allen's film *Manhattan* demonstrates how the modern, young adult who is seeking meaningful relationships may abandon traditional norms of sexual behavior and enter into multiple sexual liaisons, which may be construed as a form of genital competitive activity. In *Looking for Mr. Goodbar,* the character Keaton plays demonstrates the distorted reverse side of the modern sexual dilemma. (The problem with this kind of behavior is that it frequently serves only to open the door to the psychiatrist's office.)

The second "revolution" of our times, which I like to call the gender revolution, may be offsetting this trend somewhat. Spurred by the ideology of the women's movement, the gender revolution has made it possible today for women to compete with men as equals in countless areas barred to them a mere generation ago. In sports, business, and the professions it is no longer taboo for a woman to aggressively pursue a place "at the top."

Fortunately, this very intensification of gender competition may be reducing the intensity of genital competition, at least in

some cases. Since it is now possible for women to be sexually assertive, the burden of making a sexual advance can be taken off
men. Without a doubt, however, this has had its troublesome side:
I have seen a number of men who are confused and who feel
threatened by this new behavior, not realizing that it is a freedom
being offered to them as well as to women. Those men who do realize it have profited from the knowledge that they do not have to
"score" constantly to be accepted; they do not have to "perform"
in the traditional male-genital manner, but can explore new possibilities of interaction with women, both in and out of bed.

There seems to be, therefore, a move away from purely genital competition in this decade and back to gender competition.
This trend in fact mirrors the normal pattern which individuals
undergo as they pass from childhood through puberty to adulthood. As children, we are most involved with gender competition.
As adolescents, we move into a period of heavy genital competition: we vie for the attention of the opposite sex by competing with
our same-sex friends. As we become adults, we give over many of
the facile rivalries of high school and begin to focus our competition sexually along gender rather than genital lines. Ideally, we
stop using genital sex as a means to curry favor or to prove our
femininity or virility, and begin competing with members of the
opposite sex in a more mature manner.

But I say "ideally" for a reason. For many of us, the development I have described stops in midstream, and we are stuck at
fourteen forever, unable to move beyond the self-defeating sexual
competition of adolescence. We flirt and we strive for sexual "conquests," speaking of the members of the opposite sex as if they
were not simply differently constructed versions of the same human beast, but exotic mutants sent here from regions unknown to
vex and frustrate us eternally.

I remember the case of an elderly patient of a colleague of
mine. He was in his sixties, extremely wealthy and successful, and
he spent most of his time, now that he was retired, lounging
around various Palm Beach pools, surrounded always by a bevy of
bathing beauties about one-third his age. My colleague and I
called him the Sultan of Swing.

Probably there are very few men who would not aspire to the
Sultan's kind of retirement. Yet what was it really all about?
What did it mean to him?

It meant, if you are to believe the current media reports, that the Sultan had "succeeded" beyond most of our wildest dreams. He was the ultimate genital sexual competitor. He called all the shots, he always had the glittering "prizes" right next to him, he was the envy of many men half his age.

And yet inside, he was stuck at the level of a fourteen-year-old boy. He was still a lonely adolescent, hoping by the adoption of a glamorous life-style to silence the voices that whispered to him continually, "You're a failure. You don't know how to perform."

The Sultan came to my colleague because he was, in his own words, "fed up with it all." It's not hard to see why. He had succeeded in buying his way into the inner circle of genital sexual fantasy, yet he had not succeeded in buying the real affection that this fantasy was supposed to represent and that he craved.

As in so many other competitive areas, winning for the Sultan had actually turned out to be a hollow loss.

9

THE SWEAT OF OUR BROWS:
Competition in the Work Place

When Adam and Eve, in the Biblical story, were banished from Paradise for having eaten of the Tree of Knowledge, they became aware of their own nakedness, their own sexual vulnerability. Perhaps the battle of the sexes began at just this moment. But something else began too—something fully as important as sexual awareness in determining the scope and quality of human life. It was that the two exiles became, for the first time, *laborers.* They discovered that the earth did not owe them a living; in the words of Genesis, we all must earn our keep "by the sweat of our brows."

This primal curse, whether you see it as legend or fact, has had a tremendous effect on our lives. The fact that most adults must work for their livelihoods means that labor has assumed a kind of necessary dignity in our eyes. In nearly all cultures, men and women have thought, and still think, that work is not only a duty but a curiously stern pleasure: making a virtue of necessity, we have come to see labor as one of the central definitions of humanness, and have in many cases wrapped our entire identities, both personal and public, up in it. So involved do some of us become in our jobs that we sacrifice friends and family to them as on some ancient altar to Need. We turn the Biblical curse into a blessing, and when we are deprived of the right to toil for a living, many of us cannot adjust to the shock of inactivity—be it in the form of unemployment, vacations, or retirement. So crucial is work to our self-concept that we often equate employment with mental health and the absence of it with sickness, or "dis-ease."

We have evolved, therefore, from a situation in which work was considered an unfortunate obligation to one in which it is considered a psychological necessity. When we are working, we like to tell ourselves, we are "gainfully" employed; when we are not, we are "shiftless bums." Recent surveys of unemployed people on welfare have shown a consistent pattern of responses to questions about self-concept and unemployment: almost unanimously they agree that, even if it meant less money, they would rather work than be idle.

This has led to a situation in which competition for employment, especially in times of economic retrenchment, can be severe. In a society in which a certain low level of unemployment is always expected, competition for the jobs that do exist can pervade all aspects of our lives; having or not having a job, in a culture which places such value on employment, can mean the difference between self-esteem and self-hatred, and so it is not at all surprising to find people competing strenuously with each other for the right to work.

This is obviously related to the high value attached to making money, but it is also related to an elementary feeling we have about ourselves: working makes us feel good. Social scientists have observed that within six months of the onset of an economic recession an increase in mental hospital admissions and suicide can be expected.

From Sweat to Threat

Psychologically, everybody wants to work. Practically, this has never been possible. We can visualize this situation by imagining the jobhunters clustered around the foot of a tall pyramid-shaped ladder with a wide base but a much narrower top. Obviously, the jobs at the bottom of the economic ladder are relatively easier to obtain, while those with greater pay and prestige are much more difficult to come by. Yet even the bottom-rung jobs, you must remember, are not available to everyone; about 5 percent of the population will be unable to get any jobs at all. These are the chronically unemployed, whose support falls to the state and whose egos and sense of themselves suffer grievously in the process.

Directly aggressive tactics frequently play a part in the process of competing for jobs. This may not be perceived by either the winners or the losers. How many times have you heard someone denounce an ethnic or racial group on the ground that they are "out to get our jobs"? One of the most important underlying reasons for such bias is the fear of economic competition: the fear, that is, that "they" will push me off the bottom of the job ladder and start advancing toward the top. When prejudice against new groups becomes endemic, discrimination becomes institutionalized and a range of Dagish tools are brought to bear on the competitive situation to ensure the continued dominance of one group over another: bullying, threats, and outright physical harassment may accompany the so-called open-market competition for jobs.

Competition for jobs is already fraught with so much anxiety that the threat of an expanded field of competitors often proves psychologically to be more than some jobholders can manage. Faced with the possibility of having to compete not only with their "own kind" but with newcomers, they simply modify the rules of the competition, and proclaim that it is henceforth open only to certain types of competitors—those, for example, with only the "right" skin color or sex.

This cuts down on the field, and seems to lend stability to the competitive situation. At the same time, it allows nervous competitors to identify with a comfortably wider structure than themselves: with a group which, like them, is perceived as beleaguered and threatened from the outside. Thus, identification with our own competitive group allows us to minimize the anxiety associated with intense job competition ("we're all in this together") and affords us a context in which we can express grievances, real or imagined, about those who seem to be out to push us down the economic ladder.

The more uncertain the economic situation, naturally, the greater the degree of anxiety regarding competition between groups and between individuals. At the same time, periods of economic stress, whether personal or societal, seem to generate a great deal of dogged determination, at least on the part of some workers. Anxiety about doing well on the job can thus be a double-edged sword: it makes workers feel nervous and unstable about their economic situation, yet spurs them to new activity, making them work all the harder to hold onto what they have—and to gain more. The anxious competitor may not always feel at ease, therefore; but he may well profit from his tension.

Job competition, then, is a complex matter which has to do with much more than mere qualification for the positions available. In the next section, I want to look at some of the competitive pressures and tactics which operate on the middle rungs of the job-market ladder.

What Makes Sammy Run?

In the 1950s, Budd Shulberg wrote a marvelous novel entitled *What Makes Sammy Run?* concerning the psychological problems of a young businessman obsessed with the notion of moving to the top of the corporate and social ladder. The main character's name was Sammy, and as the title of the book suggests, Shulberg strove to examine the motivations behind the need to "get ahead." I want to look now at what happens to all the Sammys of our world when they start to move up the job ladder toward positions of ever greater responsibility, prestige, and wealth.

It is naive to assume that the higher you go up the ladder, the easier things get for you. You are making more money, to be sure, but this does not necessarily mean you must be happier or more "successful." Many so-called successful people come to me for treatment, and their cases suggest that in fact the opposite is true.

First of all, as you rise up the job ladder, the pressure to compete with your peers becomes much more intense because there are fewer and fewer "plum" jobs at the top. In these higher regions, you have to become more aggressively and singlemindedly competitive simply to survive. It is not accidental that so many upper-level corporation executives develop ulcers and heart trouble at an early age: the need for them to compete daily to hold a competitive edge over their peers and the greater responsibility of their positions dictate that such stress-related diseases be more common among them than they are among the population at large.

Secondly, when more responsibility is assumed, the pressure to perform (and to compete in performing) also increases. This is not always psychologically satisfying.

And finally, the higher you go in a corporate structure, the more closely you must identify your personal goals with the goals of the organization for which you work. The assembly-line worker need not feel any connection at all between his or her dreams and the designs of the company at large, but the executive who does not feel such a connection—and give solid evidence of feeling it—will soon find himself or herself slipping down the ladder. (The self-employed entrepreneur is confronted with a different kind of problem. For him, competition is primarily directed to the outside and he thus experiences a different set of pressures. If he is an autocomper, he may also feel internal pressures to meet various goals. But he will usually slip down the ladder only if his business fails.)

Many workers are forced to place the goals of their companies above their own personal goals, at least for a period, as a way of proving their "loyalty" and thus bettering their chances of advancement. A worker, at almost any point on the ladder, may be required to make personal sacrifices of time which he or she would prefer to spend with family or friends, and these sacrifices may—often do—precipitate marital strife. The worker may also experience considerable anxiety and personal insecurity if the company falls on hard times, since layoffs will not be far behind. The knowledge that it may sometimes be in the competitive interest of an employer to cut back on his work force thrusts workers up and down the job ladder and leads them to recognize their ultimate expendability.

Business competition, then, can have a profound effect on the way we look at ourselves, our jobs, and our stability. What happens at the top affects all of us—though clearly it has a more immediate effect on those who are near the top. For them, group and individual competition sometimes fuse, as they allow themselves to identify their personal fortunes with the far wider fortunes of the company.

Another type of job-related anxiety occurs if the company with which top executives are connected is involved in illegal or immoral activities. Since the financial pressures of modern corporatism are so intense, many businesses have adopted a kind of cutthroat approach to their rivals. Industrial spying and sabotage, the overlooking of poor design or dangerous workmanship (as was alleged in recent cases in the American automobile and tire industry), and corruption on the international trade circuit are a few of the abuses that this competitive attitude has generated in recent years.

What happens to a person high on the corporate ladder when he or she discovers that The Company—his "second family"—has been involved in shady practices? He can blow the whistle and lose his job—a bad competitive move, though perhaps a good moral one. Or he can shut up, profit from the situation along with the company, and start growing ulcers. Either way, he is caught in the middle of his own competitive needs (the principal one being to keep his job) and the wider competitive needs of the company. Resolving the tension between the two can be, for many executives, a harrowing and extremely stressful problem. In the movie *The China Syndrome,* Jack Lemmon plays the character of a nuclear power plant supervisor caught in just such a bind. His blowing the whistle ultimately leads to his death.

You may wonder, then, what is so great about being up there that keeps many of us continuing to climb madly for the top. Why, in the face of all we know about how uncertain and anxiety-provoking it is at the top, do we still want to get there? What makes us Sammys climb?

It would be foolish to deny that *some* aspects about life at the top are very pleasant indeed.

There is, first of all, the money. Psychologically, this may be a mixed blessing, but it is seldom seen as mixed in a culture as avidly enamoured of high salaries and high consumption as ours is. Few of us would deny that higher pay is a principal incentive for striving to climb the job ladder, and given the steady rate of inflation these days, it is obviously not a bad one.

But it's not the only incentive, nor in my view the most significant one. Far more important than money, I believe, is the status and prestige associated with promotions and more responsible jobs. America has been called a nation of "status seekers," and this characterization is valid, not only for America but for all of today's industrial nations. In climbing the job ladder, all of us are seeking that aura of respect and approval that comes with the higher positions. Considering what we've learned about childhood influences on later competitive efforts, this may be seen as a carryover of the child's need to be loved and approved of by his parents.

A third benefit involved with rising in the world is the power and influence it gives those on the upper rungs over those on the lower. If the seeking of status is a mask for the seeking of approval, then the seeking of a position which allows you to think of yourself as superior to others is a modification of the need for control. That this need is a central and pervasive element in the hierarchies of many job situations is evidenced by the prevalence of the barnyard term "pecking order" to describe what goes on between the members on higher and lower rungs of the job ladder.

A prime rule of the pecking order is that you must only peck down, never up; indeed, much of the criticism that comes from "on high" in corporate structures is passed on down the line as a way of alleviating the pressure and anxiety of being pecked on by the top brass in the first place. Unconsciously, we say to ourselves: "My boss just insulted and wronged me. But I'll feel a lot better if I insult and wrong the guy just below me." Like all animals, we humans seem to have a need to assert dominance over each other. It's doubtful that if the pecking order in corporate barnyards (as Vance Packard called it) were to vanish tomorrow, there would be quite as many junior execs bucking for the top honcho's spot: the opportunity to vent your frustrations is an important attraction of the higher posts, and clearly many of us feel that that opportunity is well worth competing for.

Executive Vertigo

As you rise up the job ladder, then, you generally experience both an intensification of satisfaction and an intensification of stress. And the higher up you go, the more prone you will be to nervousness and worry—that peculiar sense of high-level anxiety that might be called "executive vertigo."

Obviously, all jobs hold a certain amount of satisfaction and a certain amount of anxiety. But for some there is a certain consolation for being lower on the scale: the dissatisfaction with making only $150 a week may be offset by the fact that when you leave work, you leave it. The executive who makes ten times this amount, by contrast, is likely to carry his work—and his worries—with him when he leaves the office. For him the anxiety generated by a more successful position serves as an impetus to seek even higher achievements. Thus anxiety is both the fuel and the price of success.

So while the benefits of competing for higher and more prestigious positions are certainly not to be denied, the wise competitor is aware that every advance in salary or status brings with it its own status-related griefs, and for some of us that is enough reason to stay where we are rather than risk a $50,000-a-year heart attack. The main point to remember when you are moving up the ladder is that if your anxiety is consistently outweighing your satisfaction, it is time to think about getting off.

As you rise, you must continually assess whether or not to proceed still higher. What you must determine in each situation is how much effort you are willing to expend to achieve a particular goal. You must ask yourself, "Can I take X amount more anxiety in order to get Y amount more job satisfaction?" If the answer is yes, then competing for the higher position is clearly in order; if it is no, then you must be able to temper your competitive strivings.

Many people have the notion that *any* raise is better than no raise at all, and that monetary advancement in the job market automatically will mean an increase in the pleasure and satisfaction with which they handle their day-to-day affairs. Nothing could be farther from the truth, as many hasty, overeager competitors have found out to their chagrin. Getting that all-important raise may prove to be more trouble than it was worth; therefore, at any point on the uphill climb, you should be willing to stop and ask yourself the question, "Is this next step worth it?" If the climb so far is blurring your vision and giving you headaches, you may have "executive vertigo"—and it may be time to slow down.

If you're stuck in a job you don't mind but don't really like, for example, but two more years at it will bring you a substantial raise and the opportunity to advance, than it's probably competitively wise to hold on for a while. If you're in a place you hate but are merely afraid to move, it might be a good idea to reassess your priorities. Remember "executive vertigo": if you're getting a great deal of anxiety and no satisfaction from your present job, it hardly matters that two years from now you'll get a chance to shift; you may well have done yourself in by then, and it may be time to consider competing for something better now.

Beating the Layoff Game

Let's assume that you are a reasonably competent, reasonably ambitious wage-earner settled into a job which seems comfortable but not entirely satisfying. Let's assume further that you have assessed the possibility of going for that raise, or that open position, or that move into the corner office, and decided that you're willing to take the chance on more stress. You're ready, in other words, to take the next step up the ladder, and you're only too aware that your competition for the next rung is stiff. What is that competition, and what can you expect from it? As you climb the ladder with the rest of us hungry Sammys, whom are you likely to meet?

In Chapter 1, you'll remember that I mentioned Fred Rojack's background as being solidly working class: unlike the Court Street crowd, he came from the other side of the tracks. Fred's father, Sam, worked in laborer's positions all his life until he achieved the position of shop foreman in the factory owned by Danny's father, Bill Marchant.

Sam went to work for Bill Marchant during the Depression, when layoffs were a common phenomenon. Some of these periodic cutbacks he survived; many he did not. But after the passing of the period of retrenchment that had brought about the layoffs he was always one of the first workers to be called back, and so gradually he rose up his job ladder to become foreman.

He did this by using a combination of competitive tools. Essentially a quiet, industrious man, Sam might best be characterized as an Indagish Bulldog (the same style, incidentally, that his son Fred eventually developed): a person who does his job well, with no questions asked, who is willing to stick to it for months or even years if he can foresee a promotion or a raise some day. Sam was an example of a type you might call the ultimate Nine-to-Fiver. In all his years of service, he was never late and took only the most essential sick days. On the job he was absolutely reliable and competent. He never involved himself with union activities, nor did he look for jobs elsewhere. In the first few years of his employment, it was natural that he should be laid off in tight periods, for he had not yet achieved any seniority. But eventually he came to be seen as a man to be counted on.

But what really clinched Sam's reputation as Old Reliable in the eyes of management was something he did that was rather uncharacteristic of him. In the late 1930s, when another layoff was just around the corner, Sam happened to submit to his foreman a design for a tool bit that could be produced a little more cheaply than the bit the company was then manufacturing. The design was appreciated, and accepted; Sam gained an immediate reputation as not only reliable, but also innovative. It thus happened that Sam was spared later on when the inevitable layoffs came.

Now, Sam had no particular desire to be a designer. It was only a fluke that led him to see how the cost of the bit could be cut. He took a chance on the idea particularly because he knew a cutback was approaching, and he knew also that his family would be sorely pressed if he was forced to join the lines of the unemployed. He assessed the situation, realized it was worthwhile taking a chance, and offered his suggestion. Since this was a competitive move against his fellow workers, he couldn't feel entirely good about it (moving up, remember, means increased anxiety), but he felt he had to try. So he utilized a new competitive tool from the center box to make his play.

The curious thing about this situation was that it was years before Sam had to submit another design to consolidate his advance. Already recognized as a good Nine-to-Fiver, he now got a reputation as an Innovator because of the single chance submission. As a result, Sam was assessed as deserving more responsibility every time the opportunity for a step up came around. He didn't have to push himself further to gain periodic promotions.

Sam profited from the assets of two of the labor force's most successful competitive types: as a Nine-to-Fiver, he established a reputation for reliability; as a sometime Innovator, he added the clout of surprise and imagination to his already solid reputation. It's not surprising that he eventually made it to foreman.

What Sam had succeeded in doing was not so much to perform his job better than the other workers on the floor as it was to present an image of himself as both a steady and an inventive member of the company "team." He had effectively packaged himself as an available, desirable product—one which the company could not refuse to keep on.

In the workaday world, we not only compete for money; we also strive to present *ourselves* as valued products to those who make the decisions about our advancement. This means that, whatever our field, we are eventually forced to sell ourselves on the basis of image and style as well as actual competence. Recognizing the importance of package, of image, then, can be a useful tool in learning how to compete on the job. In other words, it's not always good work that gets you the promotion; frequently it's the fact that your work *looks* good.

Sam's case also illustrates another important rule about competing along the job ladder. To be successful, you must not only demonstrate a good, day-to-day reliability; you must, at least in times of economic stress, be able to shift your competitive style, to take on the tools of other types of competitors, to vary your attack. The continual Innovator will not necessarily maintain respect on a day-to-day basis; the mere Nine-to-Fiver will gain nothing else. When times get tight, both are likely to be left out in the cold.

The Innovator is unlikely to be successful over the long run in any but the most eccentric kinds of positions (such as that of Idea Man for a large corporation). Indeed, some Innovators—those, for example, who show an overzealous attention to what the company is doing wrong rather than right—may simply be branded Troublemakers, and dismissed.

The Nine-to-Fiver, the good company man, has a better chance of advancing up most job ladders, especially if he or she becomes so reliable, so ready to do the company's bidding, that he begins to turn into a Workaholic. The psychological stress which results from changing to a sixty-hour-a-weeker, needless to say, can be severe. But there's no denying that if you stick with a work-yourself-to-death attitude toward your job long enough (provided you are also competent at it), the dedication will pay off.

The problem is that the true Workaholic is actually addicted to work. Like those people who use alcohol to escape from personal problems, he turns to overwork as a way to treat some other emotional disruption in his life. Subconsciously, in effect, he is saying to himself, "If I work hard enough I won't have time to deal with the problems in my marriage or other relationships. If I'm an excellent worker, maybe they'll go away." The problem is that they usually don't, and they eventually catch up with the Workaholic.

If you find yourself trying to compete with a Workaholic, remember that his Achilles heel is the inevitable disarray in his personal life. You can never put in more time than the Workaholic, but you can certainly put in better, more productive time. You must guard against his making you feel intimidated or guilty through his overwhelming involvement with the job. You cannot beat him by adopting his competitive tools. You must strive instead to use your own tools as effectively as you can.

Interdependency: The Management of Competition

Competition on the job is complicated by the fact that, in many work situations, we are not only competing with our fellow workers for promotions and raises, but forced to cooperate with them as well in order to get the job done right. This is true in all types of jobs, but it's especially so where there is actual physical contact or proximity between the workers, such as that which exists in many factory settings. Workers on an assembly line, for example, must cooperate with each other or the entire line will stop; individual competition in a setting like this is thus often subsumed under a wider competitive focus, as Line A competes with Line B for the highest monthly productivity figures.

Settings in which our ability to complete a task is based on successful cooperation between potential rivals are called positive interdependency group settings. They are quite common in industry. Settings in which interpersonal rivalry is enhanced rather than diminished by the group are called negative interdependency group settings. Such a setting might exist, for example, in a real estate office where agents are in competition with each other for sales. A mixed interdependency group setting, finally, is one in which there is a balance of cooperation and rivalry among the members of the group. If the agents in an insurance office were competing against other agents in the area for regional sales goals, for example, the staff would be positively interdependent while trying to beat out the other companies, and negatively interdependent in terms of each agent's relationship with his co-workers. Thus, the competitive atmospheres of work places vary according to which type of interdependency is dominant. Generally speaking, positive groups generate greater cooperation and less individual competition, because persons in such a setting identify strongly with the group and experience an enhanced sense of self-worth and self-esteem when the group succeeds. Although comparisons are made between individuals in the group, they tend not to be invidious.

Conversely, a negative group intensifies individual competition and diminishes cooperation because there is less identification with the group, there is a higher level of invidious comparison, and a more frequent loss of self-esteem unless one happens to be at the top of the pile. Although competition for promotions, raises, and other such prizes is always keen even in positive groups, in a negative group it is usually more intense and frequently ruthless.

Many companies use a kind of mixed interdependency group setting to promote a competition among their workers which increases productivity and profits. In large factories, where there are several crews or assembly lines working simultaneously on the same project, the management will sometimes offer prizes or bonuses to the crew which shows the highest level of achievement within a given period. This creates a positive group among the workers within each crew, and an overall negative group among the crews themselves. This system, which curiously enough is in practice in the Chinese Communist cadre system as well as in capitalist factories, generally ensures higher productivity because it enlists competitiveness for the company's (or the state's) own benefit.

Is There a Back Way Up?

By and large, Innovators, Nine-to-Fivers, and Workaholics all use direct competitive tools to get what they want. Indirect tools are, however, also commonly used in the job market, and I want to look now at a couple of our fellow climbers who choose to approach the problem of getting ahead by going, as it were, around to the back door.

The first of these is the Yes-Man.

The Yes-Man's tactics are all indirect—either Indag or Indinag. He or she uses charm, flattery, acquiescence, and even outright lying as a way of currying favor with superiors and establishing himself or herself as a good Joe or Jane who always seems to be cooperative and friendly.

As we've emphasized, all people need approval, and this is no less true of persons at the top of the ladder than at the bottom or middle. Mr. Big needs his strokes just as you need yours, and if he must get them from someone he half suspects is insincere, that's better than not getting them at all. As a result, you'll find many top executives surrounded by a bevy of sycophants whose main purpose is to give their bosses assurance that they are the creative geniuses they hope they are. That these Yes-Men are kept around is evidence that they are succeeding in the highly competitive world of upper management.

Not that they succeed on flattery alone. The indirect tools favored by the Yes-Man may secure him a sinecure somewhere near the top, but unless he has other qualities that recommend him for advancement it's unlikely that he will be able to get by indefinitely on being servile. The Yes-Man approach, in other words, seems more a reliable and temporary expedient—a way to rise toward the top—than a surefire method for staying there. Eventually, even Mr. Big will tire of hearing these repetitive accolades. You will have to prove yourself in other ways if you are to continue to be competitively successful.

It has been said that to move up as a manager you must learn to be a "first-class subordinate." That observation points to both the advantages and the disadvantages of the Yes-Man approach to advancement. The use of such indirect tools as flattery and charm may get you started up the job ladder, but it will not secure a higher position unless you demonstrate real competence in areas other than apple-polishing.

The same may be said of another kind of indirect competitor, the Cheat, who resorts to the use of unfair or illegal leverage as a way of ensuring advancement over those who may be better or equally well qualified. There are numerous ways to cheat without appearing to do so, and some competitors have perfected such methods to an art. Politicians have been especially adept in the past in securing high position through the use of such indirect tools as influence, nepotism, string-pulling, payoffs, bribes, and the like. But these practices are not, of course, confined to the political arena: espionage, blackmail, and the awarding of sexual favors is every bit as common in the business world as it is in the chambers of Capitol Hill. It would be naive to think that cheating did not frequently serve quite effectively to advance a career or secure a higher prestige position.

But cheating is a dangerous competitive tool. The Cheat cannot, by the very nature of his approach, count on much support from others; nor can he ever be sure that his tactics will not someday be found out. Like most liars, he ultimately fails to cover his tracks well enough, and is discovered. The fate of the Watergate conspirators is an example of the limits which society places on cheating as a competitive tool.

Similar to the Cheat is the Back-Stabber, who while appearing to be your ally, will not hesitate to bury you if it is in his best interest. Once you have identified them, your best defense in dealing with both of these Indagish competitors is to avoid them when possible and to use great caution when you are forced to deal with them.

A more honorable way to move up the job ladder is through the use of a mentor relationship. This is usually not a conscious ploy, but rather a chance occurrence occasioned by the older, established person's developing a special interest in the career ambitions of an unusually promising newcomer. The younger person becomes his protegé and thereby greatly improves his chances for climbing up the ladder of success. The protegé is grateful for this help and attention, for it usually serves to diminish his anxiety and increase his satisfaction. The mentor, for his part, is pleased to see the bright new star following in his footsteps.

Now, such a way of advancing sounds ideal. What, you may ask, is wrong with this competitive technique? How can it possibly fail? The problem is that the protegé inevitably will want to move in directions contrary to the desires of the mentor in order to be true to himself and to foster his own growth. As this occurs, the mentor becomes disenchanted with the protegé and withdraws his support. If the protegé has achieved a secure enough position by the time this happens, he is able to continue up the ladder on his own. Otherwise, he is forced to break away from his mentor and seek a new setting in which to nourish his own professional development.

Many strong competitors, upon reaching the summit of their aspirations, find that the top just doesn't satisfy them; others see their goals receding constantly the higher they climb on the social or economic scale. The discovery, ultimately, that "making it" is often a hollow gain is one of the most traumatic events that the successful competitor can experience.

Gloom at the Top?

In the British film *Room at the Top* the character played by Laurence Harvey feels that his life will be transformed if only he can marry an upper-class girl and get a well-paying job in the business of one of her associates. He succeeds in doing so, but in the process loses nearly everything but his paycheck. He finds, when he finally "arrives," that the top is far from the paradise he had envisioned it to be. The price he has had to pay in terms of personal dignity to get there has made him a bitter and confused old man before the age of forty; he cannot derive any genuine satisfaction from his position.

The notion, therefore, that after a certain period of time as a competitor you will suddenly and miraculously become a "happy" person, a person without problems, simply does not hold up in the real world. There may indeed be room at the top, but not room without troubles.

Since so few can reach the pinnacle, the top posts turn out to be the most precarious: there are always people on the rung just below you who want to kick you off your perch. So fluid is life at the top that several huge "headhunting" firms—executive recruitment is the polite name—now do a thriving business specializing in shuffling corporate VPs from business to business. The insecurity of these high-level jobs, of course, has a great deal to do with the intensity of competition between rival companies: a recent round of "president shifting" on the part of the three major American TV networks suggests the degree to which high-echelon jobs are linked to "ratings," closed deals, and other quasi-tangible evidences of success.

Does this mean you should refuse to compete for the top jobs? Does it mean that the stress associated with the "best" posts is so intense that no one can really call himself or herself satisfied to be there?

Obviously not. But it does suggest that, moving up the ladder, you should be willing to assess carefully just what the advantages and the disadvantages of high-level competition are. Moreover, you should be willing to make such an assessment before you are forced to decide that you will accept or reject an offer for advancement.

It means, finally, that you should be willing to consider the possibility that, in some situations, competing for a higher paying or more prestigious job may not be the right choice for you. And it means that you should be willing to make the choice *not* to compete with a clear conscience, burdened neither by guilt nor by the resentment of your fellow competitors.

Remember that as you rise up the job ladder, your satisfaction should increase rather than decrease or remain the same; if this is not happening, then it may be time to call a stop, and re-examine where you are going. It may even be time to pull out of the competitive job race altogether.

Stopping

This is what Sam Rojack finally did.

At the age of fifty-five, after having worked in the Marchant firm for half of his life, he was sized up as a good prospect for a "front office" job, and asked by Bill Marchant himself if he wouldn't like to move into the air-conditioned quarters of management. Sam thought about it for a few days, and declined the offer.

Many would think that Sam made a serious mistake in turning down the post. Not only did he reject the money involved (there was a substantial raise associated with the promotion), but he turned his back as well on the higher prestige and the many social advantages accruing to a management pick rather than a shop foreman.

In Sam's mind, however, there was no doubt that he had made the right decision. After thirty years on the shop floor, he knew the work routine well; he was comfortable with his own responsibilities and confident that he could handle any question that came his way within the context of his job. Accepting the management post would have meant more responsibility and more stress as well. Sam knew himself well enough to realize that he didn't need the extra emoluments if they had to be purchased at the price of his self-confidence and daily ease.

Sam made, in other words, a rational decision *not* to continue competing. It was a decision based neither on fear nor on confusion, but on a realistic assessment of his own capabilities and the requirements of the new position. He realized that, in spite of the many attractions of the promotion, he had already "arrived" by his own standards and didn't need a higher pay scale or a key to the executive washroom to convince himself of the fact.

Sadly, very few of us have Sam's kind of equanimity. For many of us, the more we sweat, the more we are obliged to sweat. I know a young musician, for example, who five years ago was earning about $200 a week. Today he's earning three times that amount. I asked him recently what he thought about the change.

"It must feel pretty good after years of making ends meet," I surmised.

"No," he replied. "The more you make, the more you need to make. Six hundred dollars is peanuts now."

As some of us become more and more successful in the job market, our needs and goals change in response to that success. The goal we think we wanted ten years ago may seem insignificant now that we are solvent and moving up the ladder. The goal, in other words, is constantly changing, perhaps even *receding* as we advance—and this means that, even if we reach the top, we may still to some extent look on ourselves as losers.

Some social scientists have made the interesting observation that success can often be measured not by the state of having *arrived* at a given point, but by having *traveled* a certain distance from whatever was the given starting point. Mobility is crucial to understanding why advancement remains attractive even to people who are already high on the economic ladder, for contentment may come not with the recognition that you now occupy a high rung, but with the realization of how far from your point of departure you have come to get there.

This observation may explain why Sam was content to stay where he was although a higher rung had been offered him. For a man who had started out literally at the bottom, attaining the rank of foreman was satisfaction enough, since it meant he had traveled a good way from his early starting point. It may also explain why Danny Marchant, who started out near the top, was never satisfied with his competitive achievements. If success is going beyond the point from which we began as our parents' children, then Danny had a much smaller scope for advancement than Sam, and regarded his moderate success as a lawyer as not "worthy" of the Marchant name. This meant that, even if he reached the top, he might still consider himself a loser.

In the end, the wise competitor is the person who plays the competitive game as long as it is fruitful for him to do so, and cuts out of the competition quickly when it proves to be self-defeating. Sam Rojack made this choice and never regretted it. Given the striving, gung-ho atmosphere of our modern business world, it's a choice that is exceedingly difficult to make. But if we are not to be caught in an eternal spiral of anxiety, it is a choice that many more of us will have to learn to accept.

The other important lesson to learn is to remain true to your own character. Whether dealing with a Cheat, a Yes-Man, a Workaholic, or a Nine-to-Fiver, the best way to ensure your own success is to do well that which you already know how to do. Assuming you are fully aware of your own strengths and weaknesses and your own best methods, it is wisest to continue to use them regardless of the styles or tools of your competitors. You must be flexible and ready to borrow some other tools if they seem more appropriate at any given time, but trying to assume your rival's style in an attempt to "fight fire with fire" will usually prove ineffectual. Your competition will invariably be more effective using those methods than you can ever be. Sharpen your own tools so that they can be most effective for you; this tactic will give you your best shot at winning the game, regardless of the opposition.

CONTEST OF SYMBOLS:
Competition in the Community

In foregoing the promotion to the management position he had been offered, Sam Rojack relinquished more than the higher pay and prestige which would have been associated with it. He gave up his chance to enjoy some of the symbols of achievement which, in a society devoted to outward manifestations of success, often seem as important as the achievement itself. Because he chose to stay where he was, Sam surrendered the opportunity, for example, to use the executive washroom; the chance to wear a suit rather than workclothes to work; the chance to drive a Chrysler rather than his old reliable Plymouth. All of these things would have been overt evidence that he had been accepted by a social group higher than the one in which he moved; they would have meant that he had competed successfully in the social sphere as well as the economic one.

Perhaps other people in Sam's position would have hesitated about accepting a job promotion that involved longer hours and greater responsibility as well as higher pay; many, however, might have been convinced to take the step up by the appeal of just those outward signs of success which Sam was able to resist. Few of us are as immune to the opinions of others as Sam; for most of us, what other people think of us matters a great deal, and the opportunity to increase their respect or envy of us is one we seldom hesitate to jump at—especially if by doing so we can also ensure ourselves greater financial security.

It's difficult to say sometimes whether the symbol or the achievement itself is of greater importance in the social sphere. Perhaps the runner really *is* running for the thrill of coming in first rather than the trophy; but in the social sphere, such "trophies" as fancy cars and club memberships are likely to be at least as important as the victory, since they both symbolize and codify it.

Symbols of competitive accomplishment, like all symbols, have very little value in themselves; they are coveted principally because of what they represent. The Cadillac owner may be able to convince himself that he drives a Cadillac because it has a smoother ride than most other automobiles or because the seats are more comfortable, but it's obvious from the nature of Cadillac ads that what its buyers are really purchasing is not comfort but status: specifically, they are buying the proof that they "belong," that they are members in good standing of the most prestigious social class. Their purchase of one of America's most expensive cars, in other words, is a gesture directed *outward* toward other people rather than *inward* toward themselves. The Cadillac (or the three-hundred-dollar suit, or the designer handbag) is meant to be *seen*: if it is not seen, and thus acknowledged as worthy of respect by the owner's social peers, it loses a great deal of its value.

This notion of status symbols as gestures directed outward is very important to an understanding of social competition. Aristotle said that the distinguishing characteristic of human beings is that they are *social* animals; competition, indeed, is almost by definition a social activity. Even the autocomper needs occasional external approval of his or her accomplishments, and for most of us that external approval is one of the central rewards of competition. In the family (where we learn the prototypical behavior that we will carry with us into later, more obviously "social" groupings), in school cliques, athletic teams, marital units, work forces, and the like, symbolic value is placed on certain external manifestations of group approval. A hug or a pat on the head tells us we are accepted and have won Mommy's or Grandpa's approval; a letter serves the same function for members of a school team, and a promotion or a private office operates in the same way in the job market. All of these symbols tell us that we have met the standards of the group, that we have crossed some invisible finish line to earn our stripes as group members.

Beyond that, however, group status symbols serve a contrary

and rather negative function. They not only reinforce our feelings of belonging; they also make it clear who is *not* "one of us," who is a member of a different, opposing, group. We join groups to be accepted by our peers, but also to be "one up" on those we consider outsiders, and much of the subsequent interaction between groups is a matter of macrocompetition, in which our personal competitive urges may be subsumed under the banner of a larger and more powerful grouping. Thus, group membership always looks outward: the proudly waved banner functions at the same time as a warning flag, telling all those who do not belong to keep away.

Why Do We Join Groups?

You may remember that, in the chapter on sexual competition, I spoke about a patient of mine named Lisa, a teenaged girl who used sexual promiscuity as a way of getting back at her family for what she saw as a lack of love and respect. Feeling unwanted at home, Lisa turned to a "fast crowd" in her school because it gave her the approval she could not get elsewhere. Unable to fit in or to compete with the overall school structure, she chose to align herself with the few "outsiders" whose feeling about themselves most closely mirrored her own. That these people were troublesome and socially obstructive actually reinforced their attraction for Lisa, for she felt, unconsciously, as they did—that "society" had always been against them, and that antisocial behavior was an appropriate way of retaliating.

Lisa, in other words, did exactly what was to be expected of someone in her situation. In order to compete socially, she made an ally of a group which by and large validated her own view of things, which made her feel as if she *belonged*. Once she was a member of that crowd, like many children who feel unloved, she found new self-respect — at least for a while. Socially she became acceptable and had learned to compete. Unfortunately, she had learned to substitute symbols of closeness for the true affection she missed from her family, and there was no way that these symbols could actually meet her needs.

So a sense of belonging is the first thing that people seek from affiliation with a group. If we are all competing for general community approval, for popularity, and yet only a few of us can effectively meet the standards of the norm, then one way of getting around failure is to change the rules: to compete with a limited group of peers, all of whom accept quite different values from the community at large.

"You say obedience is a virtue here? Well, I can't be obedient, so I'll join a group where disruptiveness is more highly prized."

"You say I have to be an athlete to be accepted by your group? Well, my group hates physical fitness; we get drunk seven days a week, we can't run even half a block — so that makes us better than you."

Groups, then, become surrogate families for many people whose original families have somehow let them down. This is especially evident in the case of young people, for example, who have joined the occult "family" sects that have been popular for the past couple of decades: the members of the Charles Manson "family" can be seen as frustrated children who were seeking from this surrogate father the approval they had not been able to get at home.

But the need for groups does not stop with the attainment of mutual affection and validation, and it is by no means confined to people whose parents and/or early friends have failed them. For many more of us, groups can be a way of gaining certain social advantages which otherwise would be denied us or a way of consolidating power and influence, of gaining through collective effort things which we realize we could not gain on our own.

This is most evident in the political sphere, where such "outsiders" as blacks, women, the elderly, and the Hispanic and gay communities have banded together to call attention to their problems. To the extent that these minorities have seen themselves as members of groups rather than as beleaguered individuals, they have been effective in gaining recognition and in changing discriminatory attitudes toward them. To the extent that they have remained resistant to organizational unity, they have failed to compete successfully. The lesson here is that what people get from group membership is not only a sense of belonging, but a tangible sense of power, and consequently of esteem.

From Belonging to Esteem

The psychologist Abraham Maslow has developed a theory of a hierarchy of basic human needs which includes all the necessities of a human existence, from the most elementary physical ones such as food and shelter to the more complicated psychological ones such as approval, affection, and a sense of personal worth. The needs he describes, not surprisingly, all have a competitive component: that is, they are all values which, generally speaking, are in short supply, and for which each of us must vie with our families, our peers, and the other members of society. I want to focus here on two higher level needs Maslow discusses, since they bear directly on what I have been saying about the competitive advantages of being a member of a group.

One of the highest needs is the sense of belonging of which I've just been speaking. It's clear that this is a central reason for the popularity of groups and for the frequency with which group competition absorbs individual competition in this society as well as in many others. Belonging to a group provides, above all, a sense of personal worthiness to the member, whatever his or her previous history. To the person who has never felt worthwhile before, this may come as a rich and welcome change, while to the person who already feels good about himself, it will reaffirm positive feelings. In either case, belonging to a group gives one a sense of what behavioral scientists call consensual validation, that is, the notion that everyone else in the group approves of you the way you are, simply because you are a member.

This sense of consensual validation is always strongest at times and in situations in which the group solidarity seems to be threatened by some external force. In times of stress, the consensus seems to harden and loyalty to one's "own kind" becomes a virtue of primary importance. Again, the political arena provides ample evidence of this: think of how quickly the Arab nations overcame their internal differences in the last Middle East war when they perceived Israel as imminently threatening them. As George Orwell pointed out in *1984,* nations generally need an "enemy" to reinforce their own internal solidarity.

As a psychiatrist, I have often observed the same thing about individuals: internal group cohesiveness always increases when the group is approached by an outsider. Look, for example, at Barbara's need to defend her choice of Juan-les-Pins as a vacation spot when Joan mentions going to a Club Med resort. Without that external spur, Barbara would be far less defensive of her "set" than she is; the implication that the group choice is less than ideal makes her defend her own far more vehemently than even she thinks it deserves. Thus, belonging to a group may serve not only to make up for a poor sense of self-validation, but also often makes a person who is already sure of himself behave as if he were even more cocksure than is the case.

The other highly important need on Maslow's hierarchical scale is something he calls esteem, which is founded on, but grows out of and beyond, the sense of belonging. There are two aspects to esteem: thinking well of yourself because the group does (externally motivated esteem) and thinking well of yourself independent of the group (internally motivated self-esteem). Obviously, both of these relate directly to competition, and often we tend to blend these two aspects seeking a sense of superiority to other group members.

If the need for belonging, for consensual validation, is fulfilled outwardly by the group as a whole, then the need for esteem, for eminence above the members of the group, also points outward: it suggests, as I implied in the beginning of this chapter, that the need to feel yourself better, or more respectable, than others is directly related to the need for external (rather than internal) approval.

The person who has gone beyond the simple need to belong and on to the need to feel superior reflects a common, and very tenacious, aspect of most human personalities. For beyond a certain point, we do not want to run with the pack; we want to be its leaders. Not only do we want to be accepted by our group, but we want to be elevated to the sedan chair that everyone else is carrying on their shoulders. We are not satisfied keeping up with the Joneses if all it means is that our friends will not look *down* on us. We want them to look *up*. We want to make the Joneses green with envy.

Although the sense of belonging is a necessary and even honorable status to want to attain, it may seem as if a sense of superiority is not. The desire for eminence does seem a less generous, indeed a less "social" value than the sense of group solidarity which underlies it. Yet both are actually equally important in terms of the human being's constant involvement with competition. If you'll think back to our descriptions of competition in the various arenas of human life, you'll see that a kind of tension between the two higher level needs in Maslow's hierarchy has been a constant theme of the discussion. This is not surprising, because in all humans the need for union with others, for a sense of belonging, vies constantly with the need to stand out from the group, to be a unique individual, thus creating not only the field for basic ego development but also the overall context for interaction, for society, for competition. This pattern is merely a variation of the original conflict and tension a growing child experiences when it yearns to retain the early symbiotic attachment to the mother while simultaneously feeling the urge toward separation and individuation.

To put this in the words of the social theorist David Riesman, we are both inner-directed and outer- or other-directed. We both seek private approval of ourselves and disdain it in the search for wider approval. We wish to be part of the crowd, and we wish to be in the sedan chair. The debate within us over these conflicting desires is constant, and it sets the stage for competition in many arenas:

• In the *family*, we need hugs, compliments, and other evidence that we are loved. But we also need to prove ourselves against our siblings and against our parents, and for this reason we form alliances, the better to secure both affection and esteem.
• In the *classroom*, we need to conform to peer pressure and community approval. But we also need to excel, in order to advance our academic standing and, ultimately, our careers. So we are torn constantly between a need to be the same as our friends and a need to perform which often subverts it.
• In *sports*, if we are spectators, we want our team to win, but we also focus attention on star players as surrogates for our own unacted need for eminence. If we are players, the tension between team feeling and the need to be the star of the game is even more obvious.
• In *sex*, we need the same hugs and compliments we needed as children—the strokes that tell us we are loved. But we also have an opposing need to dominate others, to prove ourselves better than our sexual partners, to score points against them and make them feel they are our conquests rather than our friends. The tension between the two is at the heart of much genital and gender competition.
• In the *workplace*, we want to be accepted as part of a good company "team" but we also need to rise up the job ladder. We need

solidarity with our fellow workers, but not at the expense of our own advancement. This causes the pecking order to be a constant aspect of our jobs.

So, in every area of competition we have mentioned, a tension between belonging and esteem is a central factor in the way competition is organized. That tension seems an essential and inescapable part of human interactions is in itself not a bad thing. In many cases, in fact, it sets up situations in which people are energized in healthy ways to compete better than they might otherwise be able to. The trouble starts, I think, somewhere around the point where the need to belong begins to give way completely to the need to establish superiority—when, in any social situation, a competitor forgets that a central need of competition is approval and begins to believe that, in the race to the top, winning, even at the expense of the group, is the only thing that matters.

Competitors who make this mistake frequently lose not only the sense of belonging which they have begun to consider unimportant, but even the sense of self-esteem for which they have sacrificed everything else. And they do so, I believe, for a consistent reason: they have lost sight of a crucial distinction between what they truly need and what the society, or their peer group, tells them that they need. In their quest for eminence, they begin to confuse goals with the mere symbols of goals, and end up taking the latter for the former.

To put it another way, they become completely outer-directed, and so cannot accurately assess their own needs any longer, because they have given over that assessment to some external authority. They forget that expensive cars and homes are only images of success, and instead make them the very goal of their competitive strivings. They begin to believe that success can be measured in symbols alone, and therefore, as they accumulate more and more of those symbols, they imagine that everyone considers them "successful." In the process, they lose sight of the core of all our competitive drives, which is the need to feel good about ourselves regardless of what the external culture tells us we should be doing, thinking, or wearing.

Images of the Core

In the competition for esteem, human beings frequently twist themselves into impossibly self-compromising knots. Thorstein

Veblen's notions of "conspicuous consumption" and "conspicuous display," which he applied to the robber baron culture of the last century, apply equally to the leisure classes of our own day. The extravagances of many Hollywood "moguls" and Arab potentates are latter-day parallels to the Kwakiutl Indian potlatches at which powerful chiefs gave away half their possessions, hoping to win public esteem through a display of extravagant wealth. Now, the social effectiveness of gestures such as these is beyond doubt. But that such examples of conspicuous display have any beneficial effect psychologically is very doubtful. They may give a veneer of self-confidence, but their use suggests that the person has lost sight of the real goals of competition and is beginning to compete for images rather than substance—because, in his highly refined world, that is all he perceives is left him.

The case of Danny Marchant is instructive. In addition to the sibling rivalry he felt for Barbara, Danny had constantly to contend with the not altogether happy fact that he was the son of an important and socially prominent family; for most of his life, he was burdened by the knowledge that he was never quite measuring up to the family image, and as a result, by the time he entered his twenties, he overcompensated wildly in an attempt to be sure that everything he did was "appropriate" to his place and station as a Marchant. This kind of compensatory social competitiveness is not uncommon.

Naturally, Danny failed to pull it off—precisely because he tried so hard. He had to belong to the "right" club. He had to drive the "right" car. He had to travel in the "right" circles. He had to buy the currently "in" paintings, or be considered (by himself, at any rate) a clod. So much energy did he put into this endeavor to secure himself a reputation as socially acceptable that he ended up an anxious, unfulfilled man, convinced that nothing he did ever quite measured up to the rigorous standards set by his father and the Marchants in general. His alcoholism, then, was related not only to his problems with Barbara and Perry, but to his more general dissatisfaction at feeling like an unsuccessful striver in their upwardly mobile set.

There's no doubt that, in some situations, status symbols such as fancy clothes and posh addresses can be a real asset competitively. The person who appears for a job interview in a T shirt and sneakers is not going to stand anywhere near as good a competitive chance as the one who comes in business attire. But the real difficulty arises when you start to confuse something like appearance, which can be an effective competitive *tool*, with the overall competitive *goals* for which you are working. Being driven in a limousine to a conference may prove to be a good competitive gimmick, and may even impress a client enough to give you that contract you're hoping for. But if the whole point of your efforts is merely to be seen, you have already started confusing shadow with substance, and should reassess your priorities before you have lost all sight of your core.

What is that core? It varies with different people, of course, but I believe that a common component of most people's competitive goals is precisely the double need we have been discussing throughout this chapter: the need to feel a sense of belonging, and the need to feel esteem. The trouble with placing a great value on such external manifestations of success as all the "right" status symbols is that they are very seductive and likely to trap you into believing they are more important than either belonging or esteem. A custom-built car, in other words, may temporarily convince you that you are worthy of respect—both other people's and your own. But that symbol is something that has been ordered for you by a commercial marketing culture, and not dictated by your own inner needs. If you allow that external force to determine your needs, you may find eventually that you have no firm sense of yourself left; all you have is images, mirror reflections of what you are supposed to look like, in a particular place and time, to be socially "in."

In short, images can help you rise up the socially competitive ladder, but unless you see them for what they are—tools rather than goals—you will probably end up paying for the confusion in other areas. The psychological tension involved in maintaining a balance between the real competitive self and the prescribed, imagistic self has sent more than one socially competitive person into deep confusion.

This is especially evident in the sphere which may be thought of as a kind of crystallization of the entire social world: politics.

From Esteem to Power

There is a common and rather quaint notion of democratic politics which sees the electoral process as a kind of open choice on the part of voters between rival theories as to how their lives ought to be run. According to this notion, politicians are seen as champions of different interpretations of the public welfare, and their desire to run for office a necessary prelude to putting their programs into effect.

There is nothing wrong with this view of politics and politicians as far as it goes, but it does little to explain why people really run for office: it doesn't, in other words, explain what needs and expectations on the part of the contestants (rather than the voters) are met by the electoral process. Yet a look at this question is central to an understanding of social competition in general, and political competition in particular.

I don't draw a firm distinction here between social and political competition, because the latter is merely, in terms of the psychology involved, a special aspect of the former. To put it more precisely, political competition is a codified and organized form of social competition, in which many of the same dynamics take place, but in which the tools, goals, and symbols of success are somewhat different.

Political success may be seen as the pinnacle of social success. The successful politician—that is, the one who gets elected—has achieved a kind of ultimate competitive victory in the social sphere: he or she has secured the fullest and, in our society, the most articulated expression of general approval and esteem. He has proved himself most "popular." Getting elected, then, satisfies for the politician the very same inner needs that are satisfied for most of us by less grandiose social accomplishments—by, for example, election to a club or acceptance by a certain social set. It's not accidental that many successful politicians serve their apprenticeship by being active in various community organizations—civic and philanthropic groups and the like. Becoming the leader of such a group fulfills on a nonpolitical level the same desires that getting elected to office fulfills on the political one: in both cases, the competition for a sense of belonging has turned into a need for more particular, individual esteem. So on a basic level, we can see political competition as merely an extension of competition between individuals and between groups first for general approval and second for eminence.

But politics has a psychological component which also makes it quite different from competition in the nonpolitical social sphere, and that is that, for most politicians, the twin needs for approval and esteem are augmented by a third, and far more driving, need: the need for influence and power. It's obvious that the motivation to get elected has something to do with a hunger for pushing through your ideas, your programs, your sense of your own self-worth, at the expense of your opponent. All of us have some interest in being carried aloft in the sedan chair; the politician wants to be able to give orders as well while he's up there.

This need for power and influence may mask a deeper need for approval, and this should lead us to look somewhat more sympathetically than is customary, perhaps, on those social lions and political giants who seem driven by a lust for power and control. Paradoxically, they may be the very people who are most in need of reassurance that they are worthwhile individuals; their yearning for the top may be seen as a transmutation of an older, and constantly unsatisfied, yearning for someone to say "You're all right."

The need for power, furthermore, seems to be a self-regenerating need. It's not only very seductive, but it can become, for the successful political climber, almost addictive. Many politicians, like entertainers, live on the sound of applause, and once they begin to hear that sound, it becomes extremely difficult for them to live without it. They may continue competing, then, not so much to further their social programs as to keep hearing the voice of general approval: they are competing, in other words, for a symbol of success rather than the chance to use that success intelligently. As peculiarly outer-directed people, they must be able to see themselves smiling in a thousand mirrors before they can believe in their own validity. Their consensual validation may have a much wider sphere than that of the members of most groups, but it has the same origin in psychological need.

Because political competition can be so addictive, it can become all-encompassing, forcing the politician to sacrifice family, friends, and health in a single-minded pursuit of "the people," which is to say his desire for popular acclaim. I have treated a number of politicians who have all attested to difficulties in their personal lives engendered by their competitive drive. And too the media frequently report on politicians with domestic troubles that can be traced to this overwhelming drive.

The Precarious Crown

"Uneasy lies the head that wears a crown." That observation, made in Shakespeare's *King Henry IV* several centuries ago, is as valid today as it was in the turbulent days of the Renaissance. While the fear of assassination may not be quite as grave or anxiety-producing today as it was in those days, it still exists and with various other insecurities forms a psychological conspiracy to make the modern politician just about as uneasy about his position as was his Elizabethan counterpart.

The pressures to which modern politicians are often subjected can be overwhelming. A campaign frequently requires that they work long hours with little sleep, little time to eat, and no time at all to relax. Since they are under constant surveillance by their opponent and by the public, they can never let down their guard, but must be continually alert. They have no certainty about success, and very little assurance that the campaign tactics that have worked last year will be equally effective this year; since these tactics (or we might say styles) vary greatly, from the direct and aggressive to the indirect and nonaggressive, the campaigning politician is in the position of a competitor who is not quite sure of the rules of the game, but is aware that they may be changing every minute. As a result, he lives throughout the campaign with a continual level of anxiety and doubt. It's not surprising that drugs and alcohol are commonly abused in this period: such substances, whatever their later addictive effects, can at least alleviate the more severe pressures of the campaign for a while.

Once elected, the politician's worries do not cease, but only take different forms. He has succeeded in convincing one constituency that he is worthy of their respect; now he must convince several new constituencies, as various pressure groups converge on him to offer their own complicated, and frequently conflicting, programs. While he may not be on the road as much as during the campaign, he must still spend long hours at work away from his family, and he must still be concerned about the potential pressures of upcoming elections. The need to maintain an image of competence and reliability while attending to the manifold problems that cause him to doubt those very qualities in himself leads many an ostensibly successful politician into a depression for which drugs and alcohol, again, often provide the only solace.

Here I am touching on what is perhaps the most deep-seated problem of the would-be politician—and it is really only a variation of what we have identified as the central difficulty of social competition at large. I mean the confusion between image and reality, or the mistaken belief that what you are showing to gain external approval is identical with what you need to feel good about yourself. Numerous politicians fall into the trap of believing their own press releases, their own campaign descriptions of themselves. They forget that competitive success in the social sphere requires a certain amount of lily-gilding, and they begin to believe that they are just as good, virtuous, hard-working, and resourceful as they must make their voters believe they are. Frequently, they end up lying to themselves as much as to their constituents, because they have allowed themselves to confuse mirror images with the real thing.

The Distorting Mirror

There is a chilling and at the same time touching moment in the German propaganda film *Triumph of the Will,* which Hitler's filmmaker Leni Riefenstahl made as a record of one of the mammoth Nazi rallies. The Führer, with his usual bombastic petulance, is exhorting the huge crowd which has gathered to hear him speak, and at his every pause they break into thunderous applause, so that he is forced to wait until the cheering subsides before he can continue.

During one of these frequent waiting periods, Hitler turns to the generals and aides gathered on the stage behind him, to see if they too are overwhelmed with the brilliance of his speech. Satisfied that they are paying him due respect, he turns again to the crowd, and for a split second the camera catches on his face an expression of utter bewilderment. At that moment, the mask of the almighty leader drops, and Hitler is revealed as a bumbling and confused child, absolutely amazed that his tirade has gotten any response at all, much less one of total approbation. "My God," he seems to be saying to himself, "I think they *like* me!"

I mention this not to excuse or justify psychologically the actions of deranged or megalomaniacal people, but to suggest that, in the most successful politicians, there is bound to be some deepseated need for approval, some unsatisfied hunger for a proof of ultimate, widespread popularity. It may not be going too far to say that politicians who win the final popularity polls, the elections, are especially in need of public approval: the need to run for office, then, may be seen as a hunger for power which in itself is a modification of an earlier and deeper need for love.

To go one step further, it might be said that those who win

elections are those who have most effectively convinced their constituencies that they are worthy of love in the first place. That is, it may not always be the "best man" who wins an election, but the one who best presents himself as a Nice Guy, or an Old Reliable, or a Solid Family Man. If the electorate votes for the person who can best serve its psychological need for a surrogate, then competitive success in politics may be expected to accrue not to the person who can do the best job, but to the one who puts on the most attractive face.

This is not the same thing as saying that all politicians are liars. Many of them no doubt truly believe their own campaign promises and would be justly shocked by the suggestion that they are dissembling. The point is that, in order to win a popularity poll, you have to prove yourself not competent so much as deserving of popularity, and in many cases this means merely that you have to remake yourself in the image of what you think your voters want to see. Hitler's Strong Man stance, then, may be seen as a mask for his own insecurities, as well as a gambit to secure allegiance from a populace that wanted a Strong Man to lead them, to stand up for them in a world forum in which it felt increasingly abused. And the Führer's expression of confusion at the rally may be seen as his own recognition that, inside, he felt like anything but a Strong Man; that he was amazed at being able to fool so many others when he could not fool himself.

Many winners of popularity polls, of course, *are* able to fool themselves, and can continue to do so for long periods of time. They see themselves being successful competitively as they adopt new public images, eventually losing sight of the fact that those images were adopted in the first place to "win friends and influence people" and not because of any intimate connection they might bear to the competitor's real needs and designs.

Public image has become so important in modern politics, in fact, that a whole new profession, that of the media expert, has come to be thought an essential aspect of any successful campaigner's arsenal. Candidates are "marketed" today, like cigarettes and soap, and the candidate who wins is very likely to be the one who looks best on camera or who looks best kissing babies, rather than the one whose ideas attract the most popular support. The *image* has replaced the *idea* as the social climber's principal marketable commodity.

Joe McGinnis, in his book *The Selling of the President,*

points out how this has worked in a couple of important American presidential elections. John Kennedy, he claims, defeated Richard Nixon in the presidential race primarily because television made him look better than his opponent: his style and appearance, rather than the things he was saying, made him the victor in the Great Debates, and thus in the final polling. Nixon himself, McGinnis says, beat Hubert Humphrey eight years later precisely because he had by then learned the importance of image, and had hired a bank of media consultants to reshape his public image from that of the somewhat sinister-looking Tricky Dick of the 1950s to the solid, reliable type the American people apparently thought of as perfect presidential timber.

The trouble with selling yourself on image rather than substance, though, is that, like the person who uses status symbols as goals rather than tools, you may end up unable to tell apart your manufactured needs from those that are truly inherent. You may find yourself in the position of the person who decks himself or herself out in a designer outfit and a high-style haircut and then looks in a mirror and is forced to ask, "Is that really *me*?"

Style is an extremely important tool in social competition, and an even more important one in political competition. But if you rely on style alone to achieve competitive success, you may well find that, although the voters or the "right" club members accept you, you have lost track of yourself in the process. All mirrors will become like distorting mirrors in a carnival fun house, as the clothes you wear and the car you drive and the smile you adopt for speeches not only "make the man" but *become* the man, in spite of yourself. The core of your competitive needs will be lost.

There is a great danger, in other words, that in social competition you will become engulfed by the many external symbols commonly employed to make climbing up the social or political ladder easier. You can get trapped by these symbols, and if that happens—if you are unable to make a realistic distinction between goals and tools—you can find youself publicly acclaimed and privately without an anchor.

And the cheer of the crowd means very little to the person who is forever lost in the fun house.

PART III
A Competitor's Primer

11

THE HEALTHY COMPETITOR:
Three Steps to Success in Competition

Because it's so easy to confuse real needs with those which the society we live in tells us we are supposed to have, many of us who are extraordinarily successful competitors in terms of social goals turn out to be failures in terms of our personal psychological imperatives. If you'll recall how several of the successful competitor's tools we discussed earlier are at best ambiguous in the light of common social morality, you'll realize why successful people are not always happy people: they have in many cases been forced, for the sake of winning the race, to employ competitive techniques which, for all their effectiveness, carry with them a great sense of guilt and questionable psychological benefit.

Take the case of Bill, for example, a corporation leader who came to me some years ago complaining that he just couldn't seem to "calm down." Constantly jittery and anxious, Bill was someone who, in the heat of the race, began confusing his own goals with those that his background and social situation had assigned him.

When he first came to me, Bill was at the top of his profession; at forty-six, he was one of the youngest company presidents in his area and had been honored many times by local civic groups for having created new jobs in the community. His business was thriving, moreover, and there was even a possibility that he would be tapped later that year to run for local office.

And yet the man was miserable.

Intensive psychotherapy revealed some of Bill's basic conflicts. As successful and hard-driving as he was, he confessed to me that, ever since he was a teenager, what he had really wanted was to run a farm. Farmers, though, had very little social prestige in the community in which he grew up, and so after graduating from college, Bill went along with the rest of his set and entered a management training program—the first step in his meteoric rise to the top.

He worked hard and was extremely well rewarded for his endeavors, but for nearly twenty-five years, he admitted, he had resented every day he had had to go to the office rather than the fields. His daily round obliged him to use competitive techniques that made him feel guilty; moreover, sitting at a desk was simply not something he wanted to be doing eight or ten hours a day.

I pointed out to Bill that, if he really hated his job that much, he could quit; he could, since he was reasonably secure financially, get a small farm any time he wanted to. But it was evident that he had been going over this same ground for so long that, by now, he wasn't sure whether he really did want to change. He had become, paradoxically, comfortable with the notion of his own frustration: in fact, it even spurred him to greater business accomplishments, almost as if he were working against himself in spite.

It took an ulcer and the threat of a heart attack to convince Bill that he was doing himself no good by choosing to compete madly in a field he had no real liking for. Eventually, he did slow down a bit, and while he never actually did get a farm, at least he allowed himself to cut down on his working hours and spend more time in his garden at home. This seemed to quiet him down a great deal; the last time I spoke to him, he had delegated a good deal of the day-to-day responsibility for running his firm to his vice-presidents, spending only three days a week at the plant. He had learned to do what he wanted to do with his days, rather than what was demanded of him because of his position.

Bill was an example of the unhealthy but successful competitor—a common specimen today. Although we are frequently reminded that "overcompetitiveness" can be bad for our psyches, from a psychological point of view there is a great deal about competitive behavior which is positive and healthy. Competition is a way of validating ourselves, of reinforcing our sense not only of survival but of self-worth and dignity. Psychologically, this more than makes up for any drawbacks inherent in competitive situations. The development of a healthy ego depends on learning how to manage the competitive interactions between ourselves and other people. Because so many human interchanges are competitive, the urge to succeed in the social arena thus becomes an important aspect of ego development, and the prevalence of competition in our society is an opportunity for growth rather than simply an impediment to some hypothetical "free" activity.

Competition, in other words, should be a boon rather than a bane to health—but this depends on whether we have a clear enough idea of how we are feeling when we compete, and whether that feeling, in the long run, is good or bad for our psyches.

What Is Healthy Competition?

While most mental health professionals seem to agree today that health is not simply the absence of disease, there is very little agreement on what constitutes health or healthy behavior, since one person's pathology may be another's sanity. As a result, it becomes very difficult to come up with a definition which will be even moderately workable in all situations.

One way of getting at what I mean by healthy competition in this book would be to give you an idea of the kinds of behavior and symptoms characteristic of unhealthy competitors. The physical symptoms are the most readily identifiable clues that there is trouble. Bill was an example of the unhealthy but successful competitor: his ulcer would have told him, even if his own dissatisfaction had not, that something in his competitive behavior was unhealthy. Heart trouble, stomach problems, alcohol or drug overuse, sexual difficulties, and chronic fatigue, insomnia, or listlessness—all of these may be associated from time to time with unhealthy forms of competitive behavior. If you suffer from one or more of these physical symptoms, your body is trying to tell you something about the way you compete. The wise competitor, no matter what his present level of "success," pays attention to such warning signs.

Beyond that, there are a host of vaguer psychological difficulties which frequently accompany unhealthy competitive behavior. These include anxiety, tension, frustration, anger, guilt, and shame experienced prior to, during, or after the competition. Again, if you are troubled by such emotional difficulties often, it may be time for you to reassess your competitive hopes, tactics, and style. All of these feelings are signals that your psyche is laboring under an undue amount of stress, and that it may be time to analyze how and why you compete.

Now, not all stress is harmful, and in fact a modest amount of anxiety may even provide a psychological boost in certain types of competition. Most athletes speak of getting "psyched up" before a game or meet, meaning that they feel themselves to have a better competitive edge when, just before the beginning of their event, they feel a little queasy, a little nervous and impatient to begin. Actors and actresses about to go on stage speak of the same phenomenon. What is commonly identified as "butterflies in the stomach" may be, therefore, a special sign of readiness rather than true anxiety; as long as the athlete or actor doesn't have to carry it with him throughout the day, it may be a welcome spur to a stronger competitive effort.

But this kind of "beneficent stress" is a special case. For the most part, the presence of stress, either chronic or acute, tells you that you are not competing in the best interests of your psychological or physical health. You may be competing compulsively, like Bill, or you may be opting out of competition because of a fear of failure, or of success. For whatever reason, if you are carrying a permanent butterfly cage inside of you, it's time to take a closer look at how you go about winning. Your own feelings about yourself, physical and emotional, are the first and truest guide as to whether or not you are competing in a healthy manner.

The healthy competitor feels good about himself or herself. He or she is not emotionally or physically constrained by competition, and enters into it in a hearty, unguilty manner, hoping and trying to win but realizing that failure is always a possibility, and that that possibility can be accepted. The healthy competitor may be quite aggressive and bold about getting ahead, but does not focus all of his or her identity on any particular competition. For the really healthy competitor, winning is the icing on the cake; the real name of the game is striving for personal excellence, win or lose.

At a marathon race some months ago, I happened to spot a rather overweight runner in the midst of a pack of much sleeker, obviously more expert runners. I watched him closely as he passed in front of the spectators, trying to get a glimpse of his face to see how being so obviously outclassed was making him react. He was being passed continually by better runners, and I thought this might be making him feel disgruntled: I expected to catch a frown, or at least an expression of physical pain.

As he approached, though, I saw that his face had an expression of utter delight. There he was, plodding along in his own markedly "unsuccessful" way, and he was radiant, exuding self-confident health. I realized that for him, as for Wanda Collins, wherever he came in in the final "scoring," he would be a winner to himself, for he was enjoying the race so much it didn't matter whether he ended up first or last. That overweight runner, intent on the *process* rather than the *goal* of his competition, was someone I would call not only healthy but successful besides—successful in his own terms.

Process and Goals

In any competitive situation, the competitor must weigh the importance of two sometimes complementary and sometimes conflicting imperatives. He must be aware of the goals he has defined for himself in the competition, and he must attend to the process of competing by which those goals are to be achieved. Balancing these elements is one of the central tasks of achieving healthy competition, and many competitors fall into unhealthy behavior patterns precisely on this account: they cannot tell the two apart, or they give so much more weight to one than the other that they end up forgetting what the race was about in the first place.

There are numerous ways to achieve a healthy balance of these two elements, and they vary considerably according to the intensity and nature of the competition. Our overweight marathon runner, for example, was engaged in a competition in which, he realized, the publicly acclaimed goal (coming in at the head of the pack) was far beyond his capacities. He chose, therefore, to give relatively little importance to this end goal, and to concentrate instead on the pleasures of running itself: since he knew he could not "win" in the conventional sense, he elected to enjoy the process of the race—and that became its own victory.

To put it another way, he saw his limits clearly and transformed what might have been a disheartening contest into a successful and healthy autocomp. In terms of balance, he succeeded in fusing the two sides of the equation to his own advantage: in making the process itself a goal.

This technique is appropriate to many autocomps, but of

course it is not suited to all competitive situations. The real estate agent who enjoys showing clients houses but has no interest in closing deals will very soon be out of a job. The tennis player who concentrates solely on "form," refusing to observe where the ball goes after he has hit it, may win a medal from the Zen Tennis Masters Association, but will not win very many matches.

Attention to process in and of itself is a necessary ingredient of competitive success, but it is not sufficient. It is even possible to become addicted to process, as the gambler becomes addicted to the peculiar intricacies of The Game rather than to the size of the potential winning. The "total-process" competitor, then, can easily become the person who competes simply for the sake of competing, without any clear notion of the goals or the reason for the game. People in this kind of situation—such as gamblers and workaholics—are unlikely to be either healthy or successful competitors in the long run.

A total dedication to goals, by the same token, can be just as damaging. Think of our young executive Bill, who spent a quarter of a century in a job he didn't really like because he believed that the goals associated with success in that job—money, prestige, acceptance—were more important than the day-to-day grind he had to go through to achieve them. Bill hated the process of his work, yet stuck with it because goals had become all-important. It's easy to see that this approach involves a serious imbalance between the two elements we've been discussing.

But knowing how to maintain a healthy balance involves a good deal of self-knowledge and self-acceptance. Indeed, these qualities are perhaps the foremost characteristics of all healthy and successful competitors. Achieving them is no easy matter, but I think the approach to achieving them—to learning how to visualize and accept yourself in any competitive situation—may be facilitated by an attention to three important steps.

Step One: Assessing Yourself

The Socratic dictum "Know thyself" is an especially useful guide for the competitor to keep in mind; without an adequate assessment of who we are, we can never hope to achieve any kind of competitive success. Knowing yourself in this sense means understanding both your particular strengths *and* your particular weaknesses. While the former are, of course, generally much easier to identify than the latter, an awareness of both, and of the ways they work together, is essential to competing well.

Knowing your strengths and weaknesses helps you decide, first of all, what kind of competitions you want to (or should) enter, and which you'd be well advised to avoid. If, for example, you've got a quick mind but no patience with detail, it's unlikely you'll make a very good bookkeeper; knowing this before you attempt to compete with people who love to handle detailed calculations may save you a lot of unnecessary stress. Most of us at one time or another enter competitions which are simply out of our league; we could cut our losses to a minimum merely by becoming aware of what we do well and what gives us trouble.

The case of Sylvia is instructive in this regard.

Sylvia was a thirty-four-year-old woman who, after ten years of marriage, divorced her husband and found herself facing the prospect of having to get a job. Her family had been quite wealthy, and during their marriage her husband had been successful enough in business so that she really didn't have to work. The only job experience she had at the time of the divorce was a year's clerical work she had done just prior to meeting her husband.

Yet because her family had been very successful socially, when it came to job-hunting Sylvia thought not of clerical work but of positions which would be more in line with her upwardly mobile background. She wanted a managerial position, but again and again was told by prospective employers that she just wasn't qualified for such a position. Sylvia insisted on ignoring their observations and pressed on with her fruitless quest.

After six months of demoralizing rejections, Sylvia decided it was time to reconsider her priorities and take a good long look at herself. She came to an important realization: the reason she had persisted in looking for a job for which she was unqualified was that she was really trying to avoid having any job at all. Naturally, after ten years of unemployment, she had developed serious doubts about her ability to hold down a job, and applying for managerial positions simply reinforced her feelings of inadequacy in this area. She realized too that the family tradition which dictated that "Women don't work" had contributed to her wariness of the job market, and had made it even easier for her to compete for work in an unhealthy and self-defeating manner.

Armed with these realizations, Sylvia took a refresher course in clerical skills at a local business school so that she could apply for jobs utilizing the strengths she had already built up. After she finished the course, she quickly obtained a position with a local corporation using these real (rather than imagined) skills. Ironically, within a short period of time she rose to precisely the kind of managerial position she had wanted in the first place.

Sylvia's case demonstrates clearly how all of us could profit from some self-analysis as a preliminary step to successful competition. Knowing what you do well and what you do not can be an invaluable initial guide in choosing the appropriate tools and the arena in which you compete.

Step Two: Setting Reasonable Goals

After you know what you can and cannot do well, the next step is to set yourself some reasonable goals. No matter how competent you may perceive yourself to be in a particular competitive field, you will not stand much chance of success if you insist on setting goals so high that they would be out of reach to any but the most brilliant competitors. Nor will you come out ahead if you consistently set mixed or conflicting goals. Your best chance of succeeding will rest on being able to predict the probable outcome of a particular competition based on a reasonable assessment of your own abilities and the apparent abilities of your rivals, and then going after a *possibly attainable* goal with all the energy and imagination you can muster. It's true that if you aim consistently low, you will only succeed in breaking even, but if you aim consistently too high, you will gain even less—and you'll end up frustrated in the bargain. "Dreaming the impossible dream" may work on Broadway, but it seldom does in real life.

Gauging an outcome, then, is a matter of weighing your own potential against the many situational variables of the particular competition in which you're interested. Your chances for success are enhanced the closer to reasonable expectations you set your goal, and diminished the closer they get to fantasy or mere wish-fulfillment. You may, for example, want desperately to get married, to find someone with whom you can share a life; and you may say to yourself that you *will* be married, come what may, by the end of the year. That is not an example of a reasonable goal.

There are so many variables associated with finding a mate that no amount of "wishing it were so" will help you compete successfully for a partner if chance and circumstances are against you.

The reasonableness of a goal is something, however, that needn't be left up to prediction or chance entirely. You have the capacity to reassess your goals periodically, and the most successful, healthiest competitors take frequent readings of their progress to see if they have overestimated or underestimated their capacities. Each new competitive situation affords you a new opportunity to do this. Therefore, competition itself can be a useful guide to further competition, for our success or failure in one event allows us to undergo a process of reality testing that is of value for our future endeavors, to see if our perceptions of ourselves within a particular competitive situation are in fact accurate. Sylvia engaged in just this kind of reality testing when she considered her repeated failures to land a managerial job; based on her findings (the dual discovery that she was assessing herself incorrectly and setting unreasonable goals), she was able to redefine what she wanted from the job market and to compete more successfully.

The closer in line with your own actual capabilities your goals are, the less likely you will be to fall into the trap of chasing truly impossible dreams, and the more likely you will be, ultimately, to feel good about yourself.

Step Three: Using Appropriate Tools

Even if you properly assess your own qualities and needs, and even if you set reasonable goals based upon them, you can still fail to compete well if you choose improper tools for getting what you want—if you persist in using tools which, although they may prove effective for other people, are not appropriate to your personal competitive style.

I have mentioned the matter of style in Chapter 3, where I pointed out that, although the best competitors frequently borrow competitive tools from quadrants other than their "own," their styles of approach tend to remain pretty constant throughout all their competitive efforts. The basically calm, deliberate Dinagish competitor may try out a flashy sport coat, for example, to impress a business client in a special situation, but it is unlikely that his entire competitive mode will ever become as flashy as the coat: he will remain a deliberate competitor momentarily disguised.

If he tries to change his entire style to go along with his new appearance, it's likely that he will fail to bring about the desired effect, for shifting styles is more difficult than it may seem at first glance. Each of us comes to be known by our peers as having a particular competitive style. It may be suave Indinag like Perry Stiles's, or flamboyant Indag like Barbara's, or dogged and straightforward Dinag like Fred Rojack's. But since these styles mirror the way we actually feel about ourselves, consciously changing them is tantamount to trying to alter our basic personality structure. That is never an easy thing to do, and indeed in some cases may be extremely unhealthy.

Even if you are not spotted immediately as a phony, you run the risk, when you change styles, of juggling with your self-image so badly that, in the midst of your competitive effort, you may lose track of where you're going, what the game is all about—even of who you are. You endanger both your goals and your health in the process.

The brief political career of Fred Rojack illustrates this point clearly. Shortly after Fred landed the Reseda job, he was elected to a city council seat by voters who were impressed by his direct, no-nonsense approach to the campaign: he told them what he wanted to do for the area and how he would go about it, and they perceived, rightly, that he meant exactly what he said. For a year, Fred served on that body with his usual undistinguished competence, fighting quietly for several public works projects which he knew would not only bring jobs into Reseda but restore some of the civic pride he had felt there as a boy. He was utterly honest, responsive to his constituency, and well liked both on the council and in the community.

But then fortune knocked on his door, and he allowed himself to undergo an unhealthy transformation. Reseda's mayor died unexpectedly, and a candidate had to be chosen to fill his place. Urged on by friends, Fred set his sights on the job. His opponent in the mayoral race was a somewhat younger, extremely well-spoken man named Renfrew. This man's speeches were not only personal and homey—they were the funniest things the folks of Reseda had heard in a political contest in years, and as popular as Fred was in the district, it was evident by the end of the first week of the campaign that Renfrew's charm was causing Fred to lose many of his old supporters.

Fred's response was uncharacteristic: he engaged a public relations consultant who told him that making over his "image" (changing his competitive style) would ensure him victory at the polls. Fred, who by this time had grown accustomed to the sound of applause and did not wish to relinquish this aspect of success, allowed the PR whiz to provide him with a new hair style, a new Italian-cut suit, and a thick book of witticisms "guaranteed" to keep the voters in stitches. By the middle of the campaign, Fred was cracking joke for joke with his opponent, and kept this up feverishly right up to election night.

And he lost by a landslide margin.

How had he managed to turn the people of his own district so solidly against him? Fred had attempted to shift from a Dinag to an Indag mode of competition. By attempting to use tools which were entirely unsuited to his style and personality, by the unwarranted assumption that what was working for his opponent would work just as well for him, Fred had undermined himself.

Had Fred stayed on his own course, he would have given Renfrew a run for his money, and perhaps even won the race. In his eagerness to be the victor, however, he forgot that he had gotten where he was by industriousness rather than wit. As soon as he started playing on his opponent's track, allowing the younger man to determine the rules, he was lost. His constituency might have been able to deal with a few minor changes, but they were so used to Old Reliable that his complete transformation utterly dismayed them: they concluded, not surprisingly, that Fred had indeed "changed"—and that he was therefore no longer reliable.

What tools should *you* use to be successful in competitive situations? Will the tools that failed Fred fail you as well? Perhaps, and perhaps not: some people compete remarkably well with the time-honored tools of deception, charm, and bumptious frivolity (though I do feel, as a psychiatrist, that there may be something unhealthy, if not unsuccessful, about this style). Only by assessing your own potentials, your own needs and drives, will you be able to determine whether you are better suited to Fred's early style, his late style—or something between the two. Just as no two people are alike, no two competitive styles are alike. It would be presumptuous of anyone to suggest that he or she knew what precise styles, what tools, what goals, would work best for you: the best you can hope for is that, by carefully appraising your past history, your qualifications for the competition, and your goals, you can be true enough to your own inner core to elicit from yourself your very best competitive efforts—that is to say, your healthiest efforts—for the situation at hand.

When you observe that your opponent is beginning to use *weapons* rather than *tools,* you know he or she is in trouble. When *you* begin to use weapons rather than tools yourself, it's time to reassess what's going on.

By a weapon I mean a competitive technique that is designed to harm another person. A tool is a technique that is designed to help you toward a better understanding of yourself, and give you a clearer notion of how to compete in a healthy way.

The distinction, I hope, is obvious. The difference between the healthy and the unhealthy competitor is simply that the unhealthy competitor believes that each competition he or she enters is a matter of life and death: the obsessive competitor enters the lists every time as if in mortal combat. The healthy competitor understands that each competition is as much process as goal, as much a ground for testing and improving himself as it is an arena for beating his opponents.

The healthy competitor realizes, finally, that there is a limit to the amount of revision you can do on your psyche and still call yourself yourself—and he or she, armed with (or, as the case may be, disarmed by) this knowledge, competes therefore with a balanced regard for the outcome. Avid as the healthy competitor may be to win, there is a final realization that not only can you not always be a winner, but that if you are constantly concerned only about becoming a winner, you will never enjoy yourself while competing.

The lesson is to stick to what you know best, to try to appreciate the process as well as the goals of your games, while remembering one important fact:

You are the only one with your style.

Avoiding Repeated Failure

Merely having your own style, of course, is no guarantee that you will be a successful competitor. It sometimes happens that we develop personal competitive styles that are actually self-defeating.

If you find yourself using a consistent set of competitive tools and a consistent competitive style, but are still failing to achieve the kinds of victories you want, it may be because you have learned to compete in an inherently unproductive way, and continue to do so not so much out of a sense of individual integrity as out of an obsessive need to go over the old familiar ground again and again. What you need in this kind of situation, obviously, is a reassessment of your qualities; you need to take a close look at yourself to see if you are "running the same loops" repetitively; you need to judge whether or not your consistency of style has turned into a detriment rather than an advantage.

Most unsuccessful competition can be traced to the competitor's failure to size himself or herself up accurately in a particular situation, and very often the unhealthy competitor is unsuccessful not only because of a current misunderstanding about his or her potentials, but because of much older patterns of unsuccessful behavior that were learned early in childhood.

Parents generally pass a legacy of competitive styles along to their children, and if the parents' ways of dealing with competition were unhealthy and unsuccessful, it's likely that their children's will be so too. Extremely aggressive competitors, for instance, often elicit unsuccessful competitive behavior in their children—as do their opposite numbers, the people who are afraid to compete at all. The children of compulsively aggressive competitors may become just as aggressive and single-minded about success as their parents, or they may react against their early role models and opt out of competition entirely. The children of passive competitors may grow up with the notion that there is something shameful about competing, and feel guilty whenever they win. In either case, the parents' own confusions about competition will have been passed on to the children, who will usually perpetuate their parents' errors.

There is a way to avoid this cycle of repeated failure, however, and that is to have the courage to evaluate your behavior on a regular basis. Such constant reassessment can help us to discern cases in which we are using competition, for example, as a way of replaying old family and in particular sibling rivalries. It can help us understand that our responses to competitive attacks are commonly grounded in the way we responded to similar attacks in our childhood—and this understanding, in turn, can help us escape the self-defeating cycle by making us realize the need for adopting new tools in new situations.

This process is anything but simple: no matter how self-defeating the old ways of competing may be, most of us are still wary of changing tools or modifying our competitive styles, simply because the old ways are known and comfortable.

What you have to aim for, when you are striving to increase your chances of competitive success, is a balance between the old tools and styles you have grown up using and the adoption of those new methods which, according to the particular competition in which you are involved, seem most appropriate.

Now, suppose you have followed all the steps for success outlined in this chapter and you still find yourself failing more often than not. What should you do?

Many people, caught in this kind of situation, go on bulldogging their way through defeat after defeat, always hoping that the next competition will prove to be the one in which the pattern changes and they see clearly the way to win. Actually, such perseverance is not always healthy—especially if you are involved in an old, repetitive pattern. Sometimes the best thing you can do is simply to withdraw from the game: to take a breather and give yourself time to reconsider your options, to reassess what you are doing wrong, and why.

The steps for competing successfully that I have talked about here can, I believe, save you from falling into the more blatant self-destructive traps which many competitors set for themselves. But they cannot really guarantee that you will be successful in all competitive situations. Chance and a host of situational variables can have a great deal to do with the outcome of any competition, and even the best prepared competitor is bound to fail sometimes. Accepting the outcome of our competitive efforts is one of the most difficult yet most important aspects of any competition. For all of us are losers once in a while; learning to live with both victory *and* defeat is perhaps the single most important psychological lesson that we need to learn to become healthy and successful competitors.

WIN OR LOSE:
Surviving the Outcome

Nobody wins all the time. The best prepared, healthiest competitor in the world is bound occasionally to miscalculate his own strengths, those of his opponent, or the nature of the competitive situation, and thus end up a loser. Because of this, it's extremely important, in terms of psychological health, for you to learn to deal with both sides of the competitive coin, to know how to be a graceful (that is, happy) loser as well as a guiltless, self-confident winner.

In the last chapter I alluded to the role luck and chance play in everyone's life. The healthy competitor knows that there is a constantly shifting aspect to competitive situations; he or she also understands that, while you cannot beat the odds, you can "rearrange" them in your favor and so give yourself an edge on your opponents, if you follow a few simple guidelines.

Increasing Your Chances

The first step toward increasing your competitive chances is, as I have already stressed, to make a cool, careful assessment of your own strengths and weaknesses, and to learn to work with the knowledge of who you really are rather than who you'd like to think you are. Many of us sleepwalk through our lives, paying very little attention to ourselves, allowing ourselves to drift in and out of situations blindly, never becoming fully conscious of how we are failing to meet our potential for winning. As a result, naturally, we frequently lose in our competitive efforts. The competitor whose chances of success are greatest is the one who constantly asks, "What am I doing now? How am I reacting to this situation? Why am I behaving like this?"

This kind of continual self-appraisal is essential to competitive health. Once you have begun to get into the habit of questioning yourself regularly, you can go on to the next step of preparation for increasing your competitive chances, and that is to measure the *costs* and *benefits* for you of any particular competition.

As we have seen frequently throughout this book, competing is not always beneficial for the people involved. There are countless ways to hurt yourself psychologically through competition, and so the healthy competitor weighs both the positive and negative possibilities of a competition before committing himself or herself to the enterprise.

The costs of a competitive effort may be monetary: the price tag may be in terms of equipment, training, or supervision. Or the costs may be measured in terms of the time or personal sacrifice you may have to make to engage in the competition: you must be able to ask yourself whether the blue ribbon you want so badly is really worth it if going after it entails spending twenty hours more a week on the job or giving up your customary weekend at the beach. Or the costs may be measured in terms of the psychological stress, the increased anxiety that is frequently a result of wholehearted competitive activity. Before entering the field, therefore, you should be willing to ask yourself if you are willing to shoulder a somewhat greater degree of possible guilt, tension, frustration, or anger than you are used to. Some people can take this in their stride, confident that winning is worth it; but many others cannot, and for them the increased burden of anxiety may outweigh the opportunity for greater success.

If you are willing to commit yourself to the competition in spite of its hazards, then your next step is to size up your opponent in much the same way that you previously sized up yourself. You should discover as many of his or her strengths and weaknesses as you can. You should know how he or she behaves in particular competitive situations. You should know which tools he or she favors, and which ones therefore might reasonably be used as countermeasures. This will allow you to anticipate his or her moves and plan your own strategy accordingly. If you know, for example, that your rival for a selling position is notoriously glib, you might want to consider using something other than your own, lesser gift of gab to impress the person who is hiring: you might want to stress your knowledge of the territory or your utter reliability instead.

Once you have sized up your opponent, you must then draft a reasonable plan of action to use in defeating him. Take a tip from the pros: you don't see the Green Bay Packers taking to the field without a thick book of game plans in mind any more than you would expect to find a successful competitor simply "winging it" through to victory. The winner generally knows in advance what his responses will be to the other fellow's moves, for he has rehearsed them thoroughly before he even entered the competition.

Having a plan, however, does not mean that you shouldn't be willing to change your notions of the contest once it has begun. You must, in other words, have not only a master plan, but several contingency plans, if you are to truly increase your chances of coming out ahead. And you must develop the ability to know when to stick to your guns (and tools) and when to switch.

Contingency plans give you an alternative to quick defeat in cases where you realize you have misjudged your own or your opponent's strengths or weaknesses. They allow you to utilize resources you might not have thought were going to be central to winning. Working out such plans to the letter is, of course, seldom possible, since even the savviest competitor can take only an informed guess as to what his opponent is going to do in the actual competition; nevertheless, having thought about alternatives to your basic approach does give you an edge over an opponent who has considered only one approach.

Finally, before you enter any competition, you should have resolved in your own mind any doubts you may have about the particular event, or about competing in general. The more ambivalent you are about the "moral" rightness of competition, the less likely you are to succeed; the more thoroughly you can commit yourself to the competition, having worked through your reservations beforehand, the more likely you are to come out a winner.

This does not mean that the winning competitor is the one who breaks all the rules in a ruthless manner. Often such recklessness simply leads to rash judgments and ultimate failure. But a half-hearted approach to competition works against both health and victory. If you have doubts about whether or not you should compete, stay out of the race. But if you decide to enter the race, you must be willing to go all out or you may as well have stayed on the sidelines. Entering, say, a political contest or a business competition with less than total commitment is like trying to run a footrace with one leg tied to the ground.

The dangers of incomplete commitment are illustrated by the story of a former patient of mine named Eric. He had gotten himself into extremely bad financial straits, and had been advised by his attorneys and accountants that the best way out of the trouble would be to declare bankruptcy. But he had strong moral scruples against what he called "living off others," and these scruples made it impossible for him to do the one thing that would have saved him from financial disaster. As a result, he spent years attempting to extricate himself from legal and monetary tangles, was in perpetual debt, and never again felt entirely comfortable about his position in the business world or the community. Although he wanted (he said) to succeed financially, he was actually only partially committed to business competition, refusing on moral grounds to use the one tool which could have brought him up from the rear. He may have felt justified in doing so, but his adamant stand against declaring himself bankrupt kept him a competitive failure most of his life.

Sabotaging Yourself

Eric's lack of flexibility in dealing with his financial situation is an example not only of how important contingency plans and commitment are to competitive success, but of how many of us go out of our way to set ourselves up for defeat, to sabotage our own efforts to succeed.

Many of us simply do not want to win. We say we want to win, but winning actually is a fearful rather than a joyous prospect to us. I mentioned earlier what behavioral scientists call the success-fearing personality; for people with such a personality structure, victory is actually seen as a defeat.

Why would a person want to lose? By and large, the fear of success has roots deep in the person's childhood, and is tied up with fear of parental disapproval, sibling rivalry, or both. I recall the case of a young woman who as a child had been consistently criticized by her parents whenever she showed more athletic ability than her brother, who was a year older. Girls were not supposed to be better athletes than boys, and so Gail learned that it was better to lose, while at the same time feeling resentful and guilty whenever she was involved in a competitive situation with her brother. She carried this constellation of ambivalent and negative feelings about winning into adulthood; by the time she was in her twenties, it had developed into a morbid fear of winning in any field at all. She subconsciously equated winning with parental disapproval and loss of parental love.

Gail had developed the art of sabotaging herself to a fine degree. She did not avoid competitions, but she made sure unconsciously that, whenever she entered one, the deck was stacked against her at the outset. She favored contests for which she was obviously ill prepared, for which she possessed none of the skills needed for victory; and she would enter these contests with neither a will nor a way to win. If the competition in question was a chemistry exam, she would wait until the last available minute to cram for the test, and always end up complaining that if only she had "three or four more hours" she would have done better.

Like many other success-fearing individuals, Gail had made procrastination the rule rather than the exception in her life, and as a result she was never properly prepared to compete. Naturally, she failed repeatedly—which was part of what she secretly wanted. But the success-fearing person also disdains losing; he or she doesn't want merely to win, but also to avoid total failure. Thus Gail was in a true psychological bind: it was impossible for her to be happy, since she didn't want to win, yet hated to lose.

Choosing competitions in which you fail continually is an almost certain sign that you harbor some underlying psychological resistance to winning, competing, or both. You may not be a full-fledged self-saboteur like Gail, but ongoing involvement in defeat suggests that you may be seeking out defeat as a way of punishing yourself for some real or imagined deficiency. If you attend to the guidelines we laid out in the previous chapter and habitually reassess your chances of victory in any given competitive situation, you ought to be able eventually to get a good idea of what kinds of competitions you should be entering and what kinds you should avoid. If, then, you often find yourself in races for which you are not suited, you should ask yourself if you are doing this as a way of reinforcing a negative self-image.

I'm not suggesting that you never enter any competition unless you are sure of victory. No one is ever *sure* of victory anyway; if you feel you have a reasonable chance even though the odds may be against you, it's perfectly healthy to give yourself the opportunity to try. But if you are consistently attracted to the types of efforts that always end up in disappointment for you, you are being neither a healthy nor a wise competitor, and you should examine whether or not you have some reason to call down punishment on yourself.

Such self-examination is also in order if you feel extreme anxiousness or nervousness in the face of potential competitions. I'm not talking about the "beneficent stress" associated with "psyching up" for an event; what I'm referring to are situations in which, even if you win, the act of competing itself elicits a whole range of negative feelings and unresolved tensions within you. The person for whom competition—win or lose—is a terrifying or nerve-wracking situation has probably not adequately assessed the psychological significance which contests have for him. Although it is possible to be a consistently successful competitor while carrying around such tensions, it is not possible at the same time to be psychologically healthy. And, as we have seen, the unhealthy competitor eventually ends up a loser.

The "Sore" Loser and the "Sure" Loser

However ardently some of us may want to fail, for most of us losing is not a great deal of fun. As a result, many defeated competitors refuse to acknowledge the fact that they have failed at all, instead concocting all kinds of stories and explanations of why the defeat was someone else's responsibility. This is especially characteristic of persons we commonly call "sore losers."

We have all run across sore losers at one time or another. They are found in every competitive arena, and they seem hellbent on making their loss just as uncomfortable for everyone else as it obviously is for them. Sometimes, like the young volleyball star Toby whom we met in Chapter 7, they will play with others only if they can be assured of being the center of attention. Sometimes, like Lucy in a recent *Charlie Brown* comic strip, they excuse their every mistake by blaming something beyond their control (in Lucy's case, it was the sun which got in her eyes every time a fly ball came her way). And sometimes they are out-and-out spoilsports, who stalk off the field of competition immediately when they perceive that they are not in complete control: the child who "takes his marbles and goes home" illustrates this kind of behavior.

Whatever form of behavior is favored by the sore loser, a consistent feature of his or her personality is that he or she cannot accept defeat as the result of performance. Sore losers must resort to rationalizations for their losses, because this is the only way they can assuage the hurt they feel when they lose.

Now, we all feel lousy when we lose, at least as an immediate reaction. What distinguishes the sore loser from the "sure" loser—the person who does not go to pieces when he fails—is that he or she has not developed any realistic ways, any workable contingency plans, for dealing with failure: all the energy of sore losers is geared to winning, and when winning does not result from their performance, they are undone.

The "sure" loser is able to make an informed and intelligent appraisal of the possibilities of victory, and can therefore react realistically in those situations where defeat is the outcome. What he or she is "sure" of is himself. The sore loser, on the other hand, overvalues the importance of every individual competition; to him, every contest is a matter of life or death, and when he loses, he has no choice but to cry "Fault!" or shift the blame elsewhere: he is so unsure of himself that he interprets every failure as proof of his basic worthlessness.

Overvaluation of competition is probably the most common underlying cause of the sore loser's reaction, but sometimes the excuses he adopts seem to indicate just the opposite: what he or she says publicly often suggests disdain for competitive effort, on quite rational and moral grounds. Upon experiencing failure in the job market, the sore loser will announce imperiously, "Money isn't everything," or "I don't want to step on people to get to the top," or "Our society's values are corrupt."

Such arguments, while they may have some basis in reality, hold little weight when they come from someone who has just been bested in the very attempt to step over other people on the way to the top. A "sour grapes" attitude, then, generally plays a crucial role in the makeup of the sore loser.

The sore loser is a tragic character on the field of competition: his elaborate denials of responsibility for his actions are not only usually transparent to others, but they actually reinforce both his feelings of negativity and the likelihood that he will continue to fail. Acknowledging failure is a necessary prelude to reassessing our strengths and weaknesses; the person who cannot do that is not likely to increase his or her competitive chances the next time around, but will remain stuck in a vicious circle of repeated failure. To deny your concern with winning or to avoid "immoral" competitive efforts almost always leads to a diminishment of your feeling of self-worth, which invariably leads to further emotional problems.

How does the sore loser get off this self-destructive merry-go-round?

The first thing must be to determine how the merry-go-round got started in the first place: he or she must find out, that is, what childhood behavior patterns form the basis of the present conduct. Sometimes the sore loser has been a pampered child who has never had to contend with the fact of loss, and for that reason has been entering adult competitions quite unprepared for anything but success. Understanding how your own particular spoilsport behavior got started is an essential first step toward correcting your impressions of winning and losing, and then eliminating the self-destructive patterns.

Unfortunately, many sore losers are extremely resistant to acknowledging that they have a problem in the first place. Admitting that they cannot deal with failure is equated, in their minds, with admitting that they *have* failed—and that is precisely what they cannot do. Often it takes the patience and counsel of friends and professionals working together to convince an inveterate spoilsport that the time has come to investigate healthier—and thus more successful—competitive modes.

Ultimately, you learn not to be a sore loser by coming to the realization that winning is not the only name of the game, and that none of us can ever win all the time. You develop the healthier qualities of the "sure" loser as you learn to derive satisfaction from your participation in the process of the game, rather than merely concentrating on the goal of winning.

This approach is valuable as well for those of us who are not sore losers. In fact, it can be quite beneficial for those who are only infrequently troubled by defeat, because winning is often as difficult to handle as losing.

Dealing with Success

It's a recognized fact that celebrities have a higher rate of emotional problems (including suicidal tendencies) than the population at large. Celebrity status—which in our culture represents the pinnacle of success—seems to bring with it a host of traumas from which the rest of the population, moderately or not at all successful, does not suffer.

Why should this be so? Why should precisely those people who have reached the top of their professions be among the most prone to self-destructive involvement in drugs and alcohol? Why should they be among those who are most attracted to suicide as a way of dealing with their problems?

According to the Horatio Alger myth, if you work hard and have good luck along the way, you will triumph over early adversities, beat out your rivals for any position you want, and attain the position most valued in our society: that of the unqualified Success. In fact, attaining success, unqualified or otherwise, is seldom as straightforward as this. I have treated numerous patients, many of them enjoying the finest fruits of official success, who would attest to the fact that "making it" is anything but a free trip to Paradise.

Inherent in the very notion of success is the fact that you have beaten out others in the race—and that fact often proves to be the psychological undoing of many a highly successful competitor. Many a winner is burdened by considerable guilt for having won out over rivals; this feeling can diminish pleasure in one's own victory.

To put it another way, the person who has succeeded well in a competitive effort is bound to have elicited, at some step along the way, the envy and resentment of those in the race who have not succeeded as well. This seems an inevitable consequence of human interaction: those on high, whatever their purity of motives or the honesty of their competitive designs, are sure to be envied by those who have fallen by the wayside.

This has a deep and not altogether salutary effect on the psychologies of both the victors and the vanquished. The losers (or at least the sore losers) very often indulge in escapist rationalizations to explain why they have been beaten, and at the same time focus a great deal of their resentment on those they see as responsible for their defeat. The victors, on the other hand, have to contend with the fact that, although they have carried away the laurels, they have in the process lost the camaraderie, the pre-competition friendships which they had hitherto enjoyed. They are no longer "one of the gang," striving for a common goal; they have become Number One, and have therefore become automatically isolated from the field in which, a short time ago, they found their most sympathetic allies.

Military people speak frequently about "the loneliness of command." The phrase is applicable as well to many nonmilitary situations, in which one person finds himself or herself suddenly raised above those who until then have been peers. A common result of being catapulted abruptly to a position of eminence is a feeling of isolation, a conviction that those who were recently your friends have somehow, overnight, become your opponents.

Highly successful competitors, for this reason, are seldom able to trust those with whom they have established long competitive contacts. Like the gunfighter in the Old West, the top dog in any competitive venture is always the standard against which the other competitors must measure their own efforts; this means that it is nearly impossible for them to relate to Number One in the same way they relate to those who have not achieved such eminence. The person on top, for his part, frequently is in the painful position of experiencing his old friends as jealous of his new power, as conspiring to unseat him, of biding their time until he makes a mistake that will give one of them a shot at the top post. His vision of his former friends as conspirators against him, moreover, is often not merely a paranoid delusion: the person at the top has good reason to suppose that he or she is the target of competitive attacks on his authority, since competition in human affairs never ceases.

The effect of this on the successful competitor's personal life is often severe. Such a person will often experience difficulty in forming close attachments; even when he does manage to do so, he may still feel wary of really opening up to his friends, for fear that underneath their affable exteriors they too are out to unseat him.

Simply because you might become successful and then be the target of envy for your peers does not mean you should refuse ever to compete. What you should do, though, is to assess sensibly what you want out of success, and what price you are willing to pay to get it. This goes back to what I said earlier about needing to weigh the costs and the benefits of competition; remembering this whenever you enter a competitive situation may help you avoid some of the more egregious hazards of getting to the top of the heap. Forgetting it may mean that you turn into someone who can never be satisfied with any single victory: someone who, like the gunfighter constantly looking over his shoulder, must be ever prepared to counter another attack, ever ready to doubt a friend, to withdraw into isolation in the mistaken belief that "Winning is All."

For the person who is as nervous about holding on to his victory as the sore loser is about disguising his defeat, winning can become a kind of millstone around the neck rather than the amulet he or she hoped it would be. Balance is needed, then, in winning and losing alike; it may be less socially acceptable to be a sore loser, but psychologically it's no less painful to be a "sore winner."

Strategies for Survival

You can survive winning *and* losing if you keep in mind the guidelines I have sketched in these last two chapters. Both winners and losers can end up unhappily if they insist on overvaluing or undervaluing competition, on setting themselves up to be defeated or to be envied for their success, and on sticking with obviously counterproductive strategies for winning. The wise, or healthy, competitor avoids these pitfalls, focusing on what he or she *personally* can do to ensure balance in the competition, even if there can never be absolute assurance of success.

Balance, in fact, may be thought of as a central key to competitive success. I have spoken before of the essential balance, in any competitive structure, between process and goals. It's just as important, psychologically speaking, to be able to balance the types of competitive tools you use, your need for affection and your need for eminence, and your individual strengths with your recognized need for help from family, friends, and others.

We all seek both security and esteem. The best way to achieve these occasionally contradictory goals at the same time is to practice balancing the above necessities. By weighing your various needs against each other, you will eventually come to understand the nature of your particular personality—and this is the only thing that can make you a truly healthy, successful competitor.

I cannot provide neat guidelines for becoming more successful in your office, in the boudoir, or on the tennis courts. All I can do is point out some general principles for you to follow in clarifying your *own* needs and designs, and hope that you will seek them out in the balanced and controlled way I am suggesting.

Ultimately, the choice of how to compete, and of whether to compete at all, is your own. Making that choice should be easier once you have fully understood the need to balance strategies, tools, and needs. Attaining that balance is an aspect of developing what has been referred to as the *observant ego*—a generally hidden part of all our personalities which nevertheless has the capacity of ensuring us both imaginative variety in our competitive efforts and security.

The Observant Ego: Your Personal Security Guard

At the beginning of this book, I asked that you keep in mind four questions whenever you found yourself in a competitive situation. I'd like you to think about those four questions again now, for they are central to the notion of developing the observant ego. You may remember that I asked you to first imagine yourself in a one-to-one relationship with another person, and then pose the following questions:

1. What is this person really saying?
2. How is it making me feel?
3. Why is he or she saying it to me?
4. How is it making him or her feel?

Reexamining those questions in the light of what you've learned about competition, you can see the value of an observant ego. For without some constantly active external awareness or monitor of yourself, competition easily becomes a miasma of second guesses, deceptions, and social masks. Lacking the observant ego, you might easily believe that what your Indag rival was saying to you was, in fact, the truth; or you might mistake a mere Buccaneer for a Bully.

The virtue of the observant ego is that it enables you to cut through the surface presentations of your rivals (and of yourself) to the heart of the competitiveness beneath. Furthermore, it can help you see all the relationships within a competitive structure as parts of a larger and less self-centered game.

The Russian mystic Gurdjieff spoke some decades ago of the chief business of life being to remember who we are. Remembering yourself became, in his system, what enlightenment is in many Eastern systems of philosophy: a moment of ultimate fusion of process and goals, in which you are beyond competition, beyond caring whether you win or lose, because you have attained a self-confidence that defeat cannot undo.

As soon as you understand that process and goals *can* fuse, that winning and losing *can* be the same, in terms of your psychological well-being, then you have a jump on your opponents in nearly all competitive arenas. The person who is not afraid to lose, who relies on his or her observant ego to see his efforts from a wider perspective, is psychologically far healthier than the person who sacrifices everything for the sake of a gold medal. For we are all losers sometime, and the healthy competitor ultimately is the one who recognizes that better than most other people. With the aid of the observant ego, he gains an invaluable competitive tool: a sense that, since his victories matter no more—and no less—than those of anyone else in the end, he could win or lose and still think of himself as a winner.

The observant ego is that part of yourself which sits back and watches your actions from the corner of the room. It's the part that is continually asking the four questions I just proposed. It's the *objective* aspect of your self, the part that can truly assess you during competitive performances, accurately describe what you're doing wrong, and tell you how to change. It's also the part that tells you, when you're on a dangerous course, that it might be the better part of valor to stop and get off.

It's the part of your personality, in other words, that is conceptually in control of the rest. It may not dictate *what* you do, but it understands your actions. And understanding, finally, is the essential ingredient in all competitive endeavors.

BEYOND COMPETITION?
Taking Your Competitive Temperature

Competition may be pervasive in human affairs, but it is anything but generally accepted. The competitive urge seems to be one of those ambiguous aspects of human personality that we grudgingly accept because we feel there is nothing we can do to eliminate it: a quality like selfishness or aggression, which brings much shaking of heads and a final resigned sigh that "This is simply human nature."

The opportunities available in competitive situations for unhealthy and self-destructive behavior at times seem far more obvious than the opportunities for growth and self-development. We may give a great deal of public approval to the notion that competition is a necessary and beneficial social force, but in our private lives few of us seem to embrace that notion wholeheartedly. Competitiveness so often leads to enmity and ruthlessness that the advantages associated with the urge to win can be underestimated.

Socialist critics are not alone in pointing out that this urge can be shockingly negative in its consequences: even the staunchest defenders of capitalism will acknowledge that such things as bullying, vindictiveness, guile, and cheating are too often a part of human interpersonal contests. And probably even the most vocal advocates of laissez-faire economics sometimes secretly wish that it were possible to get the benefits of untrammeled competitiveness without having to pay for them in ill feelings, ulcers, and broken careers.

But is there any way to accomplish this? Is there a way to forego or avoid the ill effects of the urge to win, to successfully encourage cooperation rather than winning at all costs, to arrange our social interactions so that we are not mired in competition, but are able to move beyond it?

The question goes back to one we raised at the beginning of this book. Is competition innate in the human beast, or is it something that can be bred or trained out of us? Is the urge to win, in other words, a matter of nature or of nurture?

As we saw in Chapter 2, humans are not alone in competing for the things they think they need. All animals in one way or another are in competition with each other for food, shelter, mates, territory, and prestige. Darwin's observations on the survival of the fittest in nature apply to humans as well, and for this reason it's perhaps unavoidable that a certain level of basic competitiveness be thought of as part of what we call "human nature."

The difficulty arises when the goals we compete for become more complicated than the goals of our fellow animals. It's one thing to admit that four people stranded on a desert island with limited food and water will naturally become rivals with one another; it's quite another to explain why, in our modern societies, people so often vie intensely with each other for such intangible goals as status and community approval.

Tangible physical goals, in other words, are easier to justify than nonphysical ones, and since most human competitiveness seems to be focused on achieving nonphysical goals, we can easily become frustrated trying to identify the attainment of the latter as part of an overall need for "survival." A status wardrobe may be extremely important to you, but it would be hard to prove that it was as essential psychologically as food is physically.

One of the things that distinguish us from the other animals, then, is the variety and complexity of our goals. Because of this, human competitiveness serves many functions that animal competitiveness does not. Most importantly, it serves certain psychological functions that are simply superfluous elsewhere in the animal kingdom, since animals' psyches are apparently less flexible and less in need of pampering than our own. Competition may begin, in the human infant, for the same reason it begins in other animal infants: to ensure an adequate supply of food and warmth. But very soon in the human's life, that essential need gets transformed into a need for other kinds of warmth, and we find ourselves competing in ways that would be incomprehensible to most animals for such intangibles as sibling approval, acceptance by a social set, and status symbols.

The instinct for self-preservation, in other words, although it may indeed be the basis of competition, soon turns into a more complicated set of drives—and, to the human, these seem just as important as the primary needs. Complexity has invaded every aspect of our social lives, and at this point, if we are to understand what makes Sammy run, we must be willing to ask which of Sammy's needs *beyond* food and shelter are being met by his scramble to the top of the heap.

As I've tried to make clear throughout the preceding chapters, in most social situations we compete for the sense of love and approval normally identified with parental approval in infancy and for a sense of eminence or superiority, which is at once an outgrowth of and a repudiation of the primary need for affection. And, as we've seen in the chapters on business and social competition, this second need can often be transformed by the exigencies of the political marketplace into a more purely aggressive need for power, influence, and control.

None of these needs are "instinctual" in quite the same way that the need for food and shelter is, but they exist nonetheless in humans, and have existed for so long and in so many different cultural settings that we may be obliged to acknowledge them now as "secondary" or "implanted" social drives, every bit as crucial to our psychological health as the "primary" instincts for survival. Obviously, the "need" to drive an expensive car or to be accepted into the "right" social circles is a more complicated and contrived one than the need to eat; psychologically speaking, however, the two may very well serve a similar purpose: they promote a feeling of well-being; they allow the person to feel good about himself.

Does this mean that we are all fated to accept exactly what our own particular social milieu tells us are appropriate goals for us in given situations? Does it mean we are doomed to compete continually for everything—whether it is necessary to us or not?

Not at all. For, although competitiveness may be inevitable in human affairs, the *forms* which it takes are not. We may be doomed to fight for whatever we want, but we still have great latitude in determining just what it is we do want. The inevitable nature of the human contest may be set, but we can still set our own goals.

Certain goals, of course, are universal and unavoidable. In addition to food and shelter, we all seem to have a deep and ineradicable need for affection, for feeling close and wanted in the early days of our existence. The psychological problems that arise later in life among people who were deprived of these things early on—people, that is, who could not compete successfully for them—are testimony to the importance of winning these early "battles" for love. In addition, we may all have a kind of innate need for that special kind of approval which enhances our sense of superiority.

As we've seen, the interplay between these two essential needs, these two essential competitive goals, forms the basis of all human competition: in the home, in the classroom, on the playing field, in the bedroom, in the workplace, and in the community at large, the anxiety engendered by the conflict between the need for approval and the need to outdo our peers generates a tremendous range of competitive interactions. In all these social arenas, we must eventually learn to manage effectively the tension brought on by these two primary and conflicting competitive needs.

For some people, competition becomes not something that they must get beyond, but a way of testing and bettering themselves as they advance in years and experience. They may not be overly attracted to the more exaggerated forms of competitiveness, and may feel no need constantly to prove themselves against others; but they are not intimidated by rivalry either, and they see each new competitive situation as an opportunity to learn new skills, to better their chances, to achieve new levels of competence and inner satisfaction.

How can you join this happy crew?

Through self-understanding. We humans may not be able to get beyond competition, but we can get beyond unhealthy and unsuccessful forms of it: we can transcend the self-destructive patterns we have set up for ourselves in the past and learn to work with rather than against ourselves. If we are "destined" to compete, we may as well be good at it. And since an honest assessment of personal strengths and weaknesses is such a crucial way to begin examining your personal competitive possibilities, I have devised the Competitor's Thermometer to help you do this. Think of this tool as a way of taking your own competitive "temperature," and use it frequently—perhaps once a month—to keep tabs on how you are doing competitively, to give yourself feedback about your likelihood of health and success.

The Competitor's Thermometer

The "thermometer" actually consists of two lists of fifteen statements each. The first fifteen statements can reasonably be expected to be true of healthy, successful competitors and the second fifteen of less healthy, less successful competitors. Respond to each statement as if it applied to you personally, and rate yourself accordingly. The interpretation of the score you achieve is given at the end of List II.

I   The following statements apply to me seldom or never (0 points); sometimes (1 point); frequently or always (2 points):

1. I have clearly delineated goals.
2. I understand my own strengths.
3. I recognize my own weaknesses.
4. I take success and defeat in stride.
5. I use a balance of center-box and quadrant competitive tools.
6. In difficult situations, I borrow tools from quadrants other than my "own."
7. I carefully determine my methods of competing.
8. I am concerned about process, about *how* I compete.
9. I am comfortable in competitive situations.
10. I observe myself objectively in the midst of competitive situations.
11. I commit myself totally to my competitive endeavors.
12. I have the support of my family and friends.
13. I prepare myself fully for the competition.
14. I pay attention to my rivals' methods, strengths, and weaknesses.
15. I develop contingency plans to deal with situational variables.

II   The following statements apply to me seldom or never (2 points); sometimes (1 point); frequently or always (0 points):

1. I have great anxiety regarding competition.
2. I feel compelled to compete regardless of the odds.
3. I feel guilty when I win.
4. I feel resentful when I lose.
5. I am dissatisfied with my best efforts.
6. I feel worthless when I lose.
7. I feel envious of my rivals, win or lose.
8. I get angry when I cannot win.
9. I believe that winning is the only thing that matters.
10. I enjoy seeing my opposition suffer.
11. I am uncomfortable when others watch me compete.
12. Once I fail, I won't compete again with the same opponent in the same arena.
13. I am disappointed with my own performance.
14. I find excuses for my losses or failures.
15. I feel frustrated in competition.

After responding to the statements in both lists, you should have a total number of points ranging somewhere between 0 and 60. Here's what your particular total score means:

Less than 15 points: If you scored this low, it's likely that you have competitive problems. You may be so wary of competition that you are afraid to compete at all, or you may be so obsessed by it that your efforts, even when successful, leave you feeling tense and unsatisfied. In either case, if you have accumulated less than 15 points, it might be a good idea to take a longer look at yourself in competitive situations, and ask yourself "What am I doing wrong?" You may want to seek professional help in dealing with these problems.

15–30 points: This is the low end of the healthy competitive continuum. If you scored somewhere in this range, you probably have some minor competitive difficulties, although they are not as severe or potentially as debilitating as those of people who scored under 15 points. You may have to reexamine your goals and methods of competition to see how you can increase your chances of success, for you are still only feeling your way in the right competitive direction.

31–50 points: This is the range of normal, essentially effective competitive behavior. If you fall within this range, you probably have, like most of us, your share of competitive problems, but none that are seriously impeding your progress socially or personally. The higher the score you achieve within this range, the more successful and healthy in your competitive efforts you are likely to be.

51–60 points: A score in this range normally would indicate exceptional success in the competitive sphere. If you are a one-time Olympic medalist now running a major corporation and are experiencing no job-related stress whatsoever, congratulations! If you're not, I suggest you go over the statements again, this time trying to keep your assessments of your qualities closer to your actual behavior rather than to your ideal or imagined behavior.

Remember that the Competitor's Thermometer is only a gauge of potential health, not a predictive device or a conclusive picture of your personality. If you score 17 or 18, you should not assume that you are barely getting by: perhaps another person would answer the statements in a slightly different way and end up with a significantly higher score. Similarly, if you score 45 or 46 you should be wary of concluding that your competitive worries are over. Keep in mind that taking your competitive "temperature" is not quite the same thing as getting a full diagnosis of *all* your competitive assets and problems.

Furthermore, your strengths and weaknesses inevitably change over time, and if you are really to profit from such a test you must be willing to reassess yourself periodically, to measure improvement and new deficiencies as well as to reexamine your overall competitive style.

So don't be discouraged if you come up with a "low" score. It may indicate that you have self-awareness and a good grip on your weaknesses, and that you're willing and eager to change. Go back to the statements one by one, and see if you can determine more specifically what you are doing wrong and what you are doing right. The 2-point items, remember, are your strengths; you will want to capitalize on them. The 1-point items may indicate areas where improvement is needed. The 0-score items are your weakest areas, and recognizing them can be a major step toward increasing your chances in future competitions.

In conjunction with the Competitor's Thermometer, it is useful to return to Chapter 3 and look again at the Competitor's Tool Box. Self-understanding, again, is the key to competitive success, whatever the arena; the competitor who appreciates his or her own style, and who is willing periodically to assess his or her strengths and weaknesses by using the Competitor's Thermometer, will stand a much better chance than the average person of doing well in competitive efforts. With the aid of an observant ego, he or she too will be in the best possible position to know when to compete and when to withdraw, when to go "all out" for a prize and when to relax into the less goal-oriented situation of savoring process as much as goals.

Beyond competition? Probably not. Probably human beings have been competitive for too long and in too many different situations for it to be reasonable or even appropriate to look forward to eliminating competition altogether in our affairs. What we can hope for is that each of us in his or her own way can learn to utilize a variety of competitive tools in as effective and nondestructive a manner as possible—and so make winning less a matter of life and death and more a means of enhancing self-respect and learning skills.

Competition has been with us throughout human development, and it will continue to be with us for as long as we are human. But that does not mean we need to be its slaves. With a little practice, with a little self-knowledge and flexibility, we can learn to master the urge to win, to make it work for us rather than against us, learn to approach the games we all play with a reasonable amount of confidence, humility, and good humor. Though we may be competitive beasts, we are fortunate in not being victims of the Law of the Jungle. Unlike the other beasts of the fields, we have the capacity to alter our environment, to redirect the way in which we compete, and to learn from our past failures. The antelope which fails to outrun the lion does not get another chance; we do, and the extent to which we seize such opportunities determines how well we will compete, in all arenas, in the future.

Index